CHANGING FACES

A history of Langford Budville, Somerset, England

Published in commemoration of the Diamond Jubilee of
Her Majesty Queen Elizabeth II
June 2012

Compiled by Marjorie Stockley

with written contributions from

Gerald & Ann Brewer
Margaret Brown
Christopher Fox
Sylvia Gothard
Robert Hayes
John Lloyd MC
Mark McDermott
Keith Moore
Geoff Pike & Sue Toomey *née* Pike
Simon Ratsey
Heather Schefe
Martin Stockley
Alan Tucker
Roger Wotton

There is history in all men's lives
William Shakespeare *Henry IV* Part 2 Act III

ISBN 978 0 9567402 4 3

Printed in England by Booksprint

CONTENTS

A view of the part of the village taken in 2011 (above) and in 1989 (below) from the church tower

PREFACE AND THANKS

The catalyst for *Changing Faces* emanated from a conversation with Sarah Nutt at a drinks party my husband Martin and I organised in 2008 in order to get to know people after our arrival in Langford Budville. Sarah lives in The Old Chapel and had been given a photograph of an Anniversary group standing outside her house, dated 1916. We still have not managed to name anyone in the photograph but it whetted an appetite to try and discover more about the history of the village. I must thank Sarah for her constant support throughout the project which had its official launch in The Martlet in December 2009.

Following this, I was given, by Barbara Lawrence, an incredibly detailed account of the history of Bindon House compiled by Julia Small, former owner of the house. It formed an important piece in the historical jigsaw and encouraged me in my quest. Too long to reproduce, I have included a potted history, courtesy of the current owner Lynn Jaffa.

I also appreciated sight of Kathryn Harris' school project containing some interesting historical facts and comparisons over time.

Gerald Brewer and Valerie Pitman (*née* Brewer) – the only 2 inhabitants known to have been actually born in the village and still living here – have been an amazing inspiration and source of information and I would like to thank them for all their time and commitment.

Robert Hayes, whose ancestors lived in the village, has the largest collection of old photographs appertaining to the village and has very kindly let us share them in our quest to build up a pictorial history of the village.

Alan Tucker, who lived in the village as a small boy, attended the village school and is a cousin of Robert's, has left an incredible legacy – a detailed history of all those named on the Roll of Honour in St.Peter's Church, Langford Budville. The full account is kept for everyone to see in the Church but a resumé is included in the book.

Glyn Jones, a long-time resident in the village has produced photographs and memorabilia with particular reference to his father Aubrey and grandfather Ernest, who were village carpenters/wheelwrights and coffin makers. The exhibition he mounted at the Village Fete in 2011 was worthy of note.

Roger Wotton has provided some evocative reminiscences of his time growing up in the village.

Mark McDermott, historian and one-time resident of the village, has given his professional advice and allowed me to use his historical work on the village. He has also kindly allowed us to include his updated history of St. Peter's Church, Langford Budville.

I am indebted to Simon Ratsey (regular contributor to the *Wellington Weekly News*), who on request, has written an overall look at weather patterns in the local area since the Bronze age – weather being such an important influence on the lives of those settlers who chose to live and stay in Langford Budville.

Keith Moore, former teacher of geology, has given us a glimpse of how the terrain has influenced previous generations.

Joy Eady, former teacher at Langford Buville Church of England Primary School, shared some important school memorabilia.

Carol Tucker's mother lived in the village for some time and Carol was able to add some interesting photographs of the school and family home to the collection.

Heather Schefe has sent from Australia a very detailed analysis of her family connections with the village.

David Percy, Philip Gothard, Jennifer Perry-Jones, Christopher Fox, Clemency Fox, Colleen Sanders (*née* Western) and June Marshall (*née* Western) have all helped identify names and places from their childhood living in the village.

Amy Blackmore kindly designed the *Changing Faces* logo which has featured on the publicity associated with the project.

There have been a host of other contributors to the project and I apologise now for any omissions.

This might be the time to state that all my findings, which are now quite considerable, will be lodged at the Somerset Heritage Centre for anyone to consult in the future. The staff at the Centre have been extremely helpful during my searches and I would like to take this opportunity to thank them formally.

In Appreciation

This book could not have happened without the support of my dearest husband Martin, who has written large sections of the book and edited it all. I thank him for his resolute support and endurance throughout the three years.

I must also thank Laighton Waymouth most sincerely for being so generous with his time and for his incredible patience during the process of producing and printing this book and designing the front cover.

To all my friends and associates who have read many proofs and listened endlessly to my tales of historical discovery – a very big thank you.

Marjorie Stockley

Chapter 1 – THROUGH THE AGES
Martin Stockley

a) Langford Budville before Domesday

Although the name Langford Budville has its origins in our Saxon and Norman forebears, there are likely to have been people living on or near this spot long before those times. How long must remain a matter of speculation, but there are one or two clues from the distant past.

The Old Stone Age

Little is known of the earliest inhabitants of what we now know as Somerset, who would have been nomadic hunter-gatherers, using flint hand-axes and sheltering in caves for shelter in the winter, for example in the Mendips.

Recurrent Ice Ages drove people back towards southern Europe but as the final Ice Age drew to an end about 10-12,000 years ago humans returned again, by now employing more refined tools and hunting horse, reindeer, hare and mammoth for food. Temperatures continued to rise, Britain became separated from Ireland and Europe, forests covered the land, the open spaces, where previously large herds of horses and reindeer had roamed, shrank and men turned to alternative sources of meat found in or near the forests – pigs, boar, auroch (wild cattle), elk, red and roe deer.

The Neolithic Age

Gradually, the domestication of animals and plants had begun, indicating that a more settled lifestyle was replacing the nomadic hunter tradition, and from about 4000BC onwards this became the dominant pattern in what is known as the Neolithic or Late Stone Age. We know that such people were to be found very near Langford Budville from the discovery of Neolithic pottery fragments at Bindon Farm, as well as a large number of Neolithic flint tools near Quaking House in Milverton and at Castle near Wiveliscombe, and a Neolithic hand-axe at Whitefield, also near Wiveliscombe. (The flints, by the way, had probably been imported – perhaps from Salisbury Plain.) Better tools enabled forest clearance to facilitate cultivation, as well as providing fuel, and man's increasing mastery of the environment at this time can be seen in Somerset from the remains of the Sweet Track, a wooden trackway across the Levels dating back to c3800BC. Stone henges began to appear from around 2900BC onwards, presumably indicating some form of mystic rituals, together with new types of pottery.

The Bronze Age

Round about 2000BC, the technique for the manufacture of bronze, an alloy of copper and tin, reached Britain. We have evidence of man's presence in Langford Budville at this time from a Bronze Age axe-head recovered by the Coopers from an old stone quarry behind Croxhall, across the road from St Peter's Church.

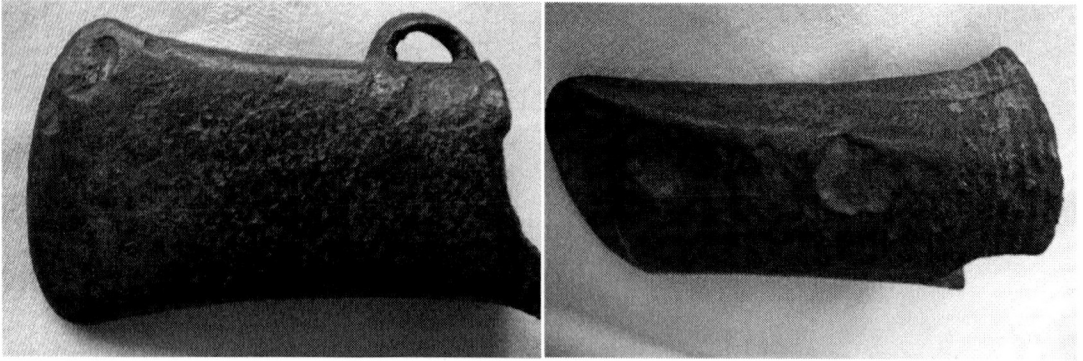

Bronze Age axe head discovered in Langford Budville in 2007.

The discovery of Bronze Age axe-heads in Milverton, a cremation urn in Wiveliscombe and both axe-heads and ornaments near Nynehead confirm the extent of man's settlement in the area.

The Iron Age

From around 650BC, the technique for the manufacture of iron was introduced from the Continent, probably coupled with periods of immigration. There seems to have been extensive settlement in the final 2-300 years before the arrival of the Romans by Celtic-speaking northern European tribes described by contemporary historians as the 'Belgae'. Certainly, by Caesar's time, the Britons were speaking Celtic languages.

The Celts brought with them not only iron, improved tools, agriculture and pottery, but also sophisticated decorative art and design concepts. Cows and sheep were farmed, pigs fattened and goats provided further supplies of milk and meat. Wheat, barley, rye and beans were cultivated in fields, usually with ditch or bank boundaries. These people were however also warlike, and Britain found itself divided into a number of often antagonistic tribal territories. West Somerset, including Langford Budville, was on the eastern fringes of the territory of the Dumnonii tribe, which extended west throughout Devon and Cornwall. Almost immediately to the east, probably just across the River Parrett, were the Durotriges, whose domain stretched from the Dorset coast up to around Bridgwater Bay. The prevalence of hill forts from these times attests to the insecurity of the population and the need for refuges when threatened, and we need look no further than Wiveliscombe to find an Iron Age hill fort at Castle.

The Romans

The Roman invasion of 43AD (Caesar's landings in south-east England in 55 and 54BC had been largely exploratory) pushed rapidly west and within a few years the military commander and future emperor Vespasian had subdued the West Country, establishing a fortress and legionary headquarters at Exeter. Soon afterwards a permanent fort was also constructed near Bodmin and, in this area, small forts were established at Norton Fitzwarren and Wiveliscombe.

The Roman Empire's motives for reaching west were probably economic – to reach and control the mineral resources found in the Mendips and the south-west peninsula, particularly tin, copper and lead – and it seems unlikely that everyday life around Langford

Budville would have been much changed by their arrival. Generally, increased demand for food from the new urban settlements and the army garrisons probably helped to ensure work for agricultural labourers, and for much of the next 350 years people lived in relative peace under the Pax Romana.

The discovery by David Cottrell of a Roman gold coin in the region of Bere Farm in the 1960s confirms the presence of a Roman influence here in our village.

Roman coin found near Bere Farm and mounted as a pendant.

Interestingly, the coin has been authenticated as bearing the head of Emperor Valens, who ruled the Eastern territories of the Empire from 364-378AD. At that time, the Empire had been split into two autonomous regions; the dividing line was approximately between Italy and the former Jugoslavia and Valens ruled the lands to the east of that line – including modern day Greece, Egypt and part of Turkey. As far as is known, he never set foot anywhere near Britain, but perhaps his coinage reached these shores via the army, whose soldiers were drawn from across the Empire and, as they were paid in cash, was a major source of currency.

The Saxons

By the early 5th century, the Roman army had departed and Britain entered a period of uncertainty with powerful local warlords attempting to exert their rule. However, the main threat to security came from the east, where raids from across the Channel and the North Sea by north Germanic tribes of Saxons, Angles and Jutes had become increasingly frequent. Within a few years, the Continental raiders had begun to settle the south and east coastal areas of England. The development of various Saxon and Anglian kingdoms in England was a lengthy and bloody business as the invaders pushed their way inland and fought among themselves for supremacy. Dominant in central southern England was the kingdom of Wessex (West Saxons), which by force of arms steadily expanded its rule further west. In 658, the West Saxon king Cenwahl defeated the British at Penselwood on the Wiltshire/Somerset border and drove them back at least as far as the River Parrett, and more likely to the hills on the Devon border (the Blackmore and Brendon Hills). Thus was Somerset brought under Saxon rule. Devon followed within about 50 years, Cornwall another 100 years later.

Although the Saxons were initially warlike, they were essentially a farming people and the land was used intensively for both crops and livestock. We do not know to what extent the indigenous population was allowed to remain living in conquered areas (probably more than was once believed) but, in any event, the language of the invaders appears to have been universally adopted and is the forerunner of modern English, as well as giving rise to most of our place-names. Langford, for example, means 'long ford' and presumably refers to the crossing over the Tone, either at Harpford or at Tonedale. (The latter seems more plausible since it better fits the description 'long', and in any case it is not clear why Harpford would have an alternative Saxon name.) Other local place names testify to our Saxon predecessors – eg Chipley means cattle-meadow, Wellisford is the ford used by the Welsh (meaning foreigners) – but tangible evidence of their presence in Langford Budville emerged in 1989 with the discovery of a Saxon burial ground next to Croxhall, opposite the Church, during excavations to build a new house. At least 10 individuals were buried here. It is thought to have been a Christian burial site, although it is not known whether there was any connection with the site of the present graveyard and Church on the other side of the road.

Langford Budville was probably less affected by the ravages of the Danes in the 9th and 10th centuries than many other parts of the country, but its people must have been at least aware of the major defeat inflicted on an invading Danish army by the combined Dorset and Somerset levies at the mouth of the River Parrett in 845. It was from Somerset, too, that King Alfred emerged from refuge in 878 to begin to drive the by now ascendant Danes out of Wessex. Whether the men of Langford Budville were conscripted to fight in these epic battles, we shall probably never know.

We do know however that before the Normans arrived in 1066 Langford had become part of the family estates of Harold, the last Anglo-Saxon King of England.

b) Normans to Tudors

The Norman Conquest

The Norman invasion of 1066 was ruthless and swift. In some ways, it was similar to the Roman conquest 1000 years earlier, in that it represented a take-over at the top rather than a re-settlement by an invading people or tribe. William I ('The Conqueror'), having seized control of the land by force of arms, proceeded to dole out the newly acquired territory to his knights as a reward for their part in the Conquest, removing the Saxon ruling class and replacing it with a French-speaking aristocracy. He then commissioned a nationwide survey of England, completed in 1086, wherein his officials visited every town, village and farmstead, assessing its ownership and value. Its purpose was to ensure that William knew down to the ultimate detail who owned what in his new kingdom and for what taxes they had been liable under his predecessor, Edward the Confessor (William did not acknowledge the legitimacy of the reign of the defeated King Harold). The assessors' decisions were final – there was no appeal – and the English named the resulting record the Domesday Book, meaning the Book of the Day of Judgement.

Langford Budville is mentioned in the Domesday Book and this fact is commemorated in a plaque on Old Post cottage.

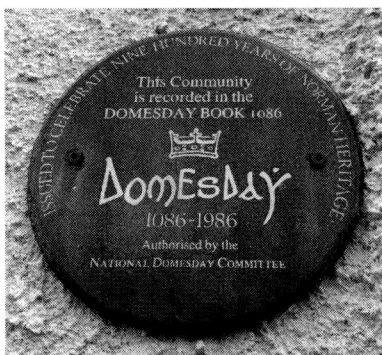

The plaque on Old Post cottage.

At the unveiling of the plaque in 1988 were Mr William Meadows, a local county councillor, Mrs Lilian Salmon, owner of Old Post cottage, Capt. John Lloyd, chairman of the parish council, Mrs Wendy Nickels, head of the village school, Robert Gothard and Kathryn Harris, the oldest and youngest pupils at the school.

The photograph appeared in Wellington Weekly News on 29th June.

This is the Domesday entry for the village:

> The King holds Langford *[Budville]*. Godwin son of Harold *[former King Harold, defeated at the battle of Hastings]* held it in the time of Edward the Confessor; it paid tax for 5 hides. There is land for 10 ploughs, of which 1½ hides are in demesne *[the Lord's private estate]* where there is 1 plough and 4 slaves; there are 21 villagers and 4 smallholders with 8 ploughs. There is a mill *[probably at Harpford]* which pays 7s 6d, 8 acres of meadow, 100 acres of pasture and 30 acres of woodland. 1 cob *[horse]*, 3 cattle, 10 pigs, 30 sheep, 18 goats. It pays £4 12s.

There are also entries for nearby Milverton, Runnington, Poleshill and Wellisford.

William made sure that land previously in the hands of the Saxon royal family became his own – even though he did not accept the legitimacy of their reign; he had no wish to see his personal stake in his new land diminished, so the manor of Langford Budville, having been previously owned by King Harold's son, was appropriated to King William I.

Mediæval Langford Budville

Some time after 1086 the manor was granted to others by the Crown, and by 1216 it was held by one Richard de Buddville, one of King John's knights. We may assume that this is how the village acquired the second part of its name, and that de Buddville was the knight of that name who had supported King John in his ill-fated efforts to retain England's possessions in France.

A church had been established in Langford Budville by at least the early 13th century (and possibly much earlier – see the section on the Saxons, above). In 1226, the chapelry of Langford Budville was presented to Bishop Jocelin of Bath and Wells by William Brewer, who at the time held the Manor of Milverton, and in 1241 the church of

Milverton, together with its associated chapelry in Langford Budville, was granted by the Bishop to the Archdeacon of Taunton. Shortly after this there was an enquiry into the death of the Chaplain of Langford Budville, who had fallen from his horse en route to Milverton.

The Archdeacon was soon to become an important landowner in the parish and remained so for the next 600 years. In 1259, Philip de Flori, who appears to have been a member of the Budville family, had been granted a carucate (approximately 100 acres) of land by his father. This area was known as Hamme, later also called Langford Flory, and is on the west side of Langford Budville towards Wellisford. On his death in 1270, Philip left this land to the Archdeacon of Taunton, Nicholas Crawford, in return for the Archdeacon committing two chaplains to pray for Philip's soul in perpetuity. (This was not an unusual stipulation in the wills of wealthy people, who hoped thereby to squeeze through the eye of the needle.) However, the Archdeacon was later obliged to assert his title in the Courts in 1275 when an Assize had to determine ownership in a dispute between him and Margery, Philip's sister. In the event, the Archbishop won his case, though Margery was excused any penalty for bringing an unsuccessful action due to her now straitened circumstances.

The Archdeacon, or his representative, was in Court again few years later in another property dispute with Robert de Harpford, presumably over land around the area of Harpford Bridge.

Meanwhile, there is a reference in 1237 to a Hugh de Wendene, also spelt Bendene and Bendone, which is believed to refer to Bindon (see separate entry for Bindon House).

The Manor of Langford Budville (the description signifies the ownership of certain rights and, usually, land, but not necessarily a specific 'manor' building) was always a relatively minor manor and the Lord thereof would have been obligated to a feudal overlord. In 1303 for example, Peter de Avesbury held Langford Budville subject to the Earl of Lincoln, an extremely important nobleman who was King Edward I's principal adviser. By 1316, The Earl of Lancaster was the superior Lord, having married Lincoln's only surviving daughter and thereby assumed all the previous Earl's rights and lands.

At the beginning of the 14th century we start to find familiar descriptions appearing in some of the surviving records of the time. The Lay Subsidy returns of 1327, recording the names of individual taxpayers and how much tax they paid, show several familiar place-names. The list for the tenants of the Manor of Langford is as follows:

Taxpayer	Amount	Comment
Willelmo de Coundenham	3s	Gundenham
Radulpho de Coundenham	2s	Gundenham
Thoma atte Wode	1s	'Wood' was a place in LB, not yet sure where
Henrico de Pynekesmore	17d	He may have lived at Bindon
Willelmo Consayl	1s	
Richardo Dawe	5d	
Roberto de Remesyet	5d	Ramsey Farm
Johanne Godeswey	10d	
Johanne de Hareford	3s	Possibly Harpford

Johanne Bruton	11d	
Johanne de Strodeshegh	15d	Stroudshey (also Stretchey). On a bend on the road to Wellisford, now just chicken runs and a few sheds
Archdeacon of Taunton	7s	A landowner in LB for over 600 years
Roberto Richeman	11d	He had been granted land in Langford Budville, including Stancombe, in 1325
Johanne Stancombe	11d	Stancombe - Johanne (Joan) was probably Rob. Richeman's wife
Roberto atte Crasse	11d	
Willelmo Terry	5d	
Roberto atte Toune	10d	
Johanne Clode	11d	There are many later references to Clode (Cload) and Clodelands. There was a Cload Cottage in the village until about 50 years ago in School Lane
Richardo Boure	1s 5d	
Richardo atte Bere	20d	Bere Farm (bearu was Anglo-Saxon for a wood)
Isabella de Bradeston	1s 5d	
Roberton atte Wode	11d	Another resident of 'Wood'
Roberto atte Mulle	11d	

The next couple of hundred years offer little by way of recorded history for Langford Budville other than various deeds attesting to property transfers. We do not know what effect momentous events such as the Black Death of 1348-9 had on the immediate area although, given that it is estimated that up to half the population of England died, it is unlikely that this village escaped unscathed. In the short term, the consequent shortage of labour enabled surviving peasants to seek higher wages, but this trend was quickly curbed by legislation that attempted to enforce pre-plague wage levels. Meanwhile, the Clode family (see table, above) continue to figure and we note later the arrival of the powerful Sydenham family as landholders in the village – although not necessarily yet as residents. The Crosse family were Lords of the Manor for much of this time.

One existing village location that may be named from these times is Butts Lane. Early in the 12th century it was made compulsory for working men to possess a bow and arrow and to keep them in good order, so as to ensure a supply of well equipped fighting men in times of war or insurrection. In the 14th century, when English archers were at their formidable peak in the famous victories over the French at Crécy and Poitiers, Edward III ordered that during holidays men should spend time practising archery. The archery target areas, or 'butts', have given rise to many place names in England and Butts Lane may have been the site of archery practice in Langford Budville. (We cannot be sure of this, however, as 'butt' was also sometimes used as a word for an abutting strip of land, often associated with mediæval field systems).

Based on some of the above records, Beatrice Swainson sketched the map below of the parish and entered on it some of the ancient place-names that are still recognisable today.

*Beatrice
Swainson's
sketch map.*

Tudor times

The Tudor dynasty ruled England from the accession of Henry VII in 1485 until the death of Elizabeth I in 1603. During this time the Manor passed from the Crosse family to the Sydenhams, who had owned land in Langford Budville since at least 1472 and later became resident in the village; the births of their children are recorded in the baptismal rolls from 1562. When Edward Sydenham of Combe, near Dulverton, died in 1543 part of his land in Langford was a plot called Tybhay. This name was very likely the origin of Tybby's (or Tibhay's) Cottage, which stood to the west of Langford Heathfield, near Poleshill, until recent times.

The Reformation of the Church, which followed Henry VIII's break with Rome in the 1530s, must have brought many changes, not all of them popular, to villages such as Langford Budville. A number of feast days were abolished since they were decreed to be "the occasion of vice and idleness", offerings to images were discouraged or prevented by the destruction of those images and parishes were urged to obtain copies of the Bible in English (previously only available in Greek or Latin). When Henry died in 1547, the pace of change accelerated. The new King, Henry's son Edward VI, was only 9 years old and was controlled by The Lord Protector, first the Duke of Somerset and then the even more extreme Duke of Northumberland, who pushed further against the traditions of the old Church. All images in churches were to be dismantled; stained glass, shrines and statues were defaced or destroyed; rood screens were cut down; vestments were prohibited and either burned or sold; church plate was to be melted down or sold; the requirement of the clergy to be celibate was lifted; processions were banned; and ashes and palms were prohibited. Chantries, means by which the saying of masses for the dead were endowed, were abolished completely. Stone altars were removed and replaced by wooden ones and an English Book of Common Prayer was introduced. It is hard to imagine the effect of all this on a society used to centuries of traditional worship and for whom the Catholic Church was a cornerstone of the community, but more confusion was to come when the next monarch, Mary Tudor, attempted to reverse all these changes and reinstate Roman Catholicism, often resorting to the most bloody repression to do so. Then, within a few years, Mary was dead and her successor and half-sister, Elizabeth 1, set about the reaffirmation of the Protestant Reformation including, in 1559, a law demanding strict attendance by all citizens at the new Anglican Church every Sunday.

Set against these turbulent times, it is some consolation that the mundane week in, week out task of maintaining the Church in Langford Budville appears to have continued largely unaffected. The Churchwardens' accounts from 1550 onwards show that outgoings were required, as ever, for new bell-ropes, greasing the bells, mending windows and battlements, washing church clothes, mending vestments (which clearly had not been discarded in Langford Budville), bread and wine for mass, maintaining the hearse, and other such normal matters. Among the more eye-catching entries were payments for the killing of pests (eg stoats or polecats, badgers and feral cats) and in 1582 payment for a 'bullock for the Queen'. This last item may have been in preparation for Anniversary Day, which was celebrated across the country on November 17th to commemorate the date of Queen Elizabeth I's accession to the throne. On the income side of the accounts, there was money received from the sale of old brass and iron, donations, and payment for reserved seats in church for the wealthier residents. Two other notable receipts were rent from the Church House and from the sale of parish ale – in respect of both of which items more will be said later in this book.

An interesting document from 1559 is the Muster Roll for Langford Budville. Muster rolls were a periodic assessment of the availability of militia that could be conscripted to act as a local defence force if needed. This is the record for the Tithing of Langford, within the Hundred of Milverton:

Ablemen

Wm. Mychell	billman	Jno. Thorne	billman
Humfry Parson	billman	Robt. Parson	archer
Wm. Holwill	archer	Xpofer Colman	archer
Nichs. Robbins	archer	Raphe Thorne	pekeman
Franke Clarke	pekeman	Jno. Persse	billman
Henry Dyrant	billman	Nichs. Chapell	billman
Mathew Wyne	billman	Nichs. Gover	billman

Armor

Within the tithing, four bills

John Syddenham, gent., one corslet furnished

Thos. Copton, one bow and one sheaf of arrows

A billman was armed with a bill, which was a 6 feet long pole with a pointed blade on the end bearing a hook which might be used to prise the enemy's armour. A pekeman (pikeman) carried a much longer weapon which could be up to 20 feet in length and bore a sharp spearhead. Note the Lord of the Manor John Syddenham's special position as an armoured gentleman. A corslet (or corselet) was a suit of light armour for the upper body. However, Syddenham seems to have been a benevolent master, for in his will of 1573 he included a provision for the poor of the village.

Also at this time the Warre family appear as major landowners in Langford Budville. (Not to be confused with the 19th century Warres of Bindon House, who had the Bindon Aisle built in St. Peter's Church). The Warres lived at Chipley Park, certainly by 1621 and perhaps much earlier than that, and the various leases they granted indicate that they had extensive land holdings in and around the village. One that has a connection today was the lease for life in 1592 of Cholwell Close to John and Mary Walrond and another party, with permission to build a house within the next three years. Cholwell has become corrupted in recent years to Chorwell, and some present day villagers can remember Chorwell Cottage, down Chorwell Lane behind Shattocks. The last building to stand there may not have been the original but it almost certainly occupied the same site.

In 1594 a copy was made of a list of the freeholders of Langford Budville who paid tax (called tenths and fifteenths) on their moveable possessions; it also recorded their property and the amount of tax due. Again, it is interesting to make the links with modern times (see facing page).

Cload Cottage, referred to in the 1594 list of taxpayers and demolished in the 20th century. A reference to Cload Cottage in 1327 presumably relates to an even older house on this site.

Freeholder	Property	Amount	Comment
Roger Cade	Ham	2s 3d	Ham was part of the Archdeacon of Taunton's lands and was a sub-manor north of Wellisford. Ham Copse still exists
Marie Woode	Tibcombe	2s 3d	Probably connected to Tybhay, later Tybby's Cottage which was not far from Poleshill
John Mill	Stancombe	15d	Stancombe is still farmed today
Nicholas Slococke	Stroudheaye	10d	Stroudshayes and Stretchey were cottages on the road to Wellisford until the last century
Jone Foweracre	Harpford	1s 3d	Always an important location, on the Tone
Robt. Carye	Gonnham	1s 3d	Gundenham
John Myll of Cholwill	Comons place	2d	Cholwill, now called Chorwell and still seen in the lane of that name. John Myll was one of several people who had a 'comons place', presumably a tenement on the common land of Langford Heathfield
John Mill	Orchardwell	1d	Orchardwell was a plot of land down the road to Runnington on the left. (Could have been the same John Myll of Cholwill)
William Mill	Ronton Downe	2d	Runnington Down
Mr Ritherdon	Ritherdons now Langford Court	13d	Roger Ritherdon (gent) also paid rates on other property
Nicholas Ewens	Middelhill	11d	Middle Hill Farm
John Birte	Bindonland	1s3d	Bindon
Thomas Autrye	Prestonorchard	2d	Possibly connected with Prestonhay field, which was between Shattocks and Oddmeads
Ambros Steare	Pulcroffe	2d	Pull Croft was a plot that ran from opposite the Church down to opposite Courtlands. Swifts was built on it
Mr Walrond	Cloadplace	15d	Cload Cottages were just down from the School, past Brockney House (see photo), although Cloadlands appears to have referred to fields on the south side of Langford Lane. John Waldron (gent) paid rates on other property and was clearly a fairly well-to-do man
Judith Crosse	Langbeare	1d	Langbeare was a field opposite Langford Heathfield, north of the Triangle

Another significant event for future generations was the arrival of the Sanford family at Nynehead in the 1590s with the acquisition of Nynehead Court and the Manor of Nynehead. Martin Sanford had married a member of the Sydenham family and the Sanfords were later to assume great prominence in Langford Budville as landowners and Lords of the Manor.

c) The 17th Century

The 17th century saw further dramatic events – the Gunpowder Plot of 1605, the Civil War of 1642-51, the execution of Charles I in 1649, the Monmouth Rebellion of 1685 – the repercussions of some of which will have been felt in Langford Budville.

Religious conformity

The Taunton area was a stronghold of Puritanism at this time. This meant virulent anti-Catholicism, regular church attendance and adherence to a pious code of personal behaviour. The records of the Archdeacon of Taunton's Court proceedings in 1623-4, as they affected Langford Budville, give a flavour:

Thomas Wygood, curate of Langford Budville, was fined 10d for negligence in his catechising and preaching.

John Fursdon and his wife were presented for not receiving Holy Communion at or since Christmas and were suspected to be recusants. They were ex-communicated.

John Richards and his wife were presented for not having received Holy Communion since Easter. They claimed to have received it at Tiverton and the minister at Tiverton was ordered to certify this.

A case against Thomazine Cape was brought for non-attendance at Church, but was dismissed when it was said that the accused had been ill.

Roger Cade and William Washer were presented for non-payment of Church dues.

The Church wardens at Langford Budville were censured for failing to provide a decent pulpit cloth.

A perhaps less strait-laced case was one of alleged Sabbath-breaking:

Twelve people had been found in the house of John Toogood, an alehouse-keeper, on a Sabbath at the time of prayer in the afternoon, and there was 'typling and drinking'. A number of the names presented will be familiar to some modern readers. In addition to the Toogoods were Nicholas Ritherdon, Andrew and Edward Greedy and the latter's wife. John Toogood and his wife claimed that they were not present themselves and it was their daughter, Anastasia, who took the rap, such as it was; she was fined 4d and ordered to confess her fault before the congregation at the end of Gospel reading. Some others were sentenced to do penance but most were dismissed with an admonition.

The said Nicholas Ritherdon seems either to have been another alehouse keeper or was very fond of 'typling', as the inventory of his possessions when he died in 1645 included 4 vats, 3 hogsheads and 5 barrels (plus 3 trundles on which to roll them)!

By the end of the century, religious conformity had been reinvested in the Anglican Church through the 1662 Act of Uniformity, although in 1689 the Act of Toleration which followed the deposal of James II acknowledged the right of dissenting sects to worship outside the established Church. These were clearly more enlightened times and it is reassuring to revisit the Langford Budville Churchwardens' accounts and note the commonplace, but laudable, purposes for which funds were deployed in 1686. Rewards were still given for the extermination of pests (including hedgehogs and foxes); financial assistance was given for the Sir John Popham Hospital Charity in Wellington, for the relief of victims of fire and for distressed former seamen and soldiers, for the repair of the stocks (which were kept in the Church grounds) and for beer money for men working on Church property.

Civil War

The Civil War arose from a whole series of incidents reflecting the mutual mistrust of Charles I and Parliament and began shortly after the King had unsuccessfully attempted to arrest a number of MPs on charges of treason. Parliament feared that Charles was scheming to invite a Catholic army to invade and in the steadily worsening relations between monarch and legislature, Parliament passed a bill in 1641 requiring all citizens to sign a Protestation swearing to uphold the Protestant faith and also to keep allegiance to the King and Parliament. The Protestation Return for Langford Budville Parish, which is of course more extensive than the village itself, lists the names of 136 men and is signed by a further 5. Women were not expressly excluded from signing the return, but some parishes, including Langford Budville, seem to have assumed that only men were required to take the pledge.

Among the names we have already encountered above were Cade, Burte (Birte), Fursdon, Gredie (Greedy), Mille (Mill), Parsons (Parson), Richards, Ritherdon, Robins (Robbins), Slococke, Thorne, Toogood, Waldron (Walrond?), Washer and Yewens (Ewens). Also listed in the Protestation Return may have been some others who had been at the 'typling' party 18 years previously: John Tose, John Goddard and William More. Further entries include George and Michael Coniber, possibly connected to the site of Coneybeare on the eastern edge of the village and Thomas Shattocke, a surname that recurs in later documents and is very likely the ultimate origin of Shattocks Cottages; another is Christopher Boober, of whom more later. However, this avowal of loyalty did not prevent the outbreak of civil war a year later.

In this area, some of the leading gentry were strongly Parliamentarian, including the Sanfords of Nynehead and the Pophams of Wellington. One can only conjecture what were the true feelings of the ordinary people. One suspects that most of them did not really have time to ponder the pros and cons of constitutional polemics, but the area was generally ill-disposed towards the Royalist central government. This was doubtless partly due to the depressed state of the woollen industry, which was a key employer here, but also because the anti-Catholic Puritan influence was strong in this part of Somerset and the King (who had married a Catholic) was suspected of sympathising with Catholicism. Henry Sanford, son of the ageing Martin Sanford and High Sheriff of Somerset, was ordered in 1640 to search the houses of suspected Royalists and Papists all over Somerset for hidden arms and material. Langford Budville did not escape his vigilance and at the house of one Master Prowse he found armour for 20 men. Interestingly, Prowse's name does not appear in either the Protestation Return of 1641/2 mentioned above, or the Lay Subsidy Roll (list of taxpayers) for the same year. One can only assume that he had been dealt with – one way or another. Henry Sanford later led a large Parliamentary force in a confrontation with Royalists at Shepton Mallet after which the Royalists withdrew; he was pardoned by the King in 1644 but died in the same year. It was he who married a Mary Ayshford and bought that name into the family.

The Monmouth Rebellion

The Monmouth Rebellion of 1685 is sometimes described as the West Country Rebellion, as it had its strongest area of support in South-West England. The Duke of Monmouth was an illegitimate son of King Charles II (of whom it was once said that he was the father of his people – at least of a good many of them). He had hoped to succeed his father as King, but when the King died in 1685, Charles's younger brother, James Stuart, acceded to the throne as James II. Monmouth decided to contest the succession by force and many Englishmen were sympathetic since James was a Catholic, whereas Monmouth was a Protestant. He landed in Dorset with a small force of barely 80 supporters but had correctly calculated that he would draw widespread support from the strongly Protestant south-west. By the time he reached Axminster he had amassed an army of 6,000 men, many of them artisans and farm workers – some with armed with no more than pitchforks. He continued to seek support, but after several weeks of inconclusive skirmishing and roaming around Somerset, he was cornered in Bridgwater and his army finally routed at the nearby Battle of Sedgemoor. Monmouth fled but was captured near Andover and subsequently executed. It is very likely that men of Langford Budville were involved in this rebellion. Certainly the authorities believed so, as the Constable's Presentments of names intended for the Assizes and Judge Jeffreys' report to King James make clear.

Wanted from Langford Budville were:

    Christopher Bodley
    John Brock
    William Brock
    Ambrose Hogley
    Humphrey Hogley
    John Hogley
    Samuel Pasmore
    John Winter

However, from the point of view of the prosecuting authorities, the village was not a productive source of guilty parties, since six of the above eight men could not be traced and the two that were presented were pardoned. Either the missing six had successfully kept their heads down, or they had been killed in engagements with the King's troops.

One imagines that the village was not too sorry to see the back of Chistopher Bodley, listed above, who seems to have been something of a bad lot. A look at some of the Justices' Court records reveals that in 1653 he had been accused of breaking into the parish pound (an enclosure for stray, or sometimes common grazed, livestock). In 1661 he was before the magistrates again, accused of coming with others to Jane Carter's house, demanding beer and striking Mrs Carter. The lady alleged that she then left the men for a while, but on returning found her chamber door broken open, her leather purse containing 15 shillings was missing and the accused were all drinking from a barrel in her chamber. Another of the accused was John Goddard, who may possibly have been the same John Goddard who had shown a fondness for 'typling' in 1623 (above).

Employment

Mention has been made of the importance of the woollen industry in this part of Somerset. Indeed, it was a vital part of the economy in many other parts of the country and the government was anxious to sustain it against imports and substitute fabrics. For centuries, the dead had been wrapped in a linen shroud prior to burial, but in 1666 and again in 1678 the Burial in Woollen Acts decreed that all deceased persons were to be buried in a woollen shroud (this legislation was not repealed until 1814, although it had been largely ignored for some years prior to that date). Such protection of the wool industry would be welcomed in Langford Budville, where there was serge-weaving on domestic handlooms in the 17th century. English weaving expertise was enhanced by the influx of Protestant Huguenots fleeing religious persecution in France towards the end of the 17th century. Some of these refugees settled in Somerset and in 1694 a collection of £1 11s 5d was made in Langford Budville "for the relief of French Protestants." However, a sign of tough times may have been the fact that John Stone, serge-maker of Langford Budville, was fined £2 in 1699 for breach of the game laws (presumably he was poaching). £1 of the fine went to the informant and the other £1 to the poor of the parish.

While the inhabitants of Langford Budville have for most of its existence laboured on the land, John Stone's trade shows that there was now some cottage industry in the village. It has also been reported that a red-earthenware pottery kiln was operating here in the late 16th to early 17th centuries.

The Rich…

The Manor of Langford Budville was sold in 1637 by the Sydenham family to brothers Hugh and John Crosse, and later in the century it changed hands several more times. However, apart from the Sydenhams and John Crosse, it seems unlikely that any of the other Lords of the Manor actually resided in Langford Budville. The other better-off residents can be identified from the Lay Subsidy Rolls of 1641 which recorded, like those of 1327 and 1594 seen above, the tax value of individual householders' properties. The wealthier inhabitants by this measure were:

Householder	Rate
John Parsons	£4 4s 6d
William Mill	£1 5s 6d
William Cade	£1 3s 6d
Mrs Elizabeth Ritherdon	£1 0s 6d
Edward Warr	16s 6d
William Thomas	16s 6d
Ames Baker	15s 6d
Robert Chave	11s 6d

Among the wealthy arrivals in the area in 1652 was Edward Clarke, who settled at Chipley and whose descendants were 100 years later to become Lords of the Manor of Langford Budville. Another family were the Havilands, who acquired Gundenham in

1687 and made it their seat for nearly 150 years. The Havilands are well represented in memorial stones set in the floor of St Peters Church.

…and the Poor

The Poor Laws had been codified in late Tudor times and were an attempt to distinguish between the impotent poor – those who for reasons of age or infirmity could not work, and the able poor – those who, it appeared, would not work. The former were to be afforded some form of relief, while the latter were to be punished for idleness. The administration of these laws fell to the Parish, who levied a tax on residents for funds to pay out to the deserving poor, while they could commit the idle poor to a period in custody or the stocks. The responsibility for vagrant beggars lay with their Parish of origin, so it was customary to give them minimal succour before moving them on towards their ultimate destination as quickly as possible and before they became a financial burden on their temporary hosts.

The authorities, in this case the Justices, were also required to deal with issues arising in connection with the maintenance of illegitimate children among the poor. So in 1615, Christopher Boobyer (of Kittisford, but possibly Boober of Langford Budville by the time of the 1641 Protestation Return, above) was ordered to maintain his bastard child by Mary Roe of Langford Budville; Mary was 'to do penance'. The following year a Certificate was lodged from Langford Budville confirming that Chistopher Bowbier (sic) had given surety for the maintenance of his child by Mary Kinge. Hopefully, this was the same Mary (perhaps she had either married or separated in the meantime) and the same child, but in any event Mary was to be put into the house of correction for one year.

The 'house of correction' may have been the Church House. Although in 1619 permission was given by Nicholas Sydenham, the Lord of the Manor, for the erection of a parochial Poor House to accommodate paupers, it is unclear whether this was ever carried out and there is some evidence that the Church House, believed to be situated immediately to the west of the Church, was used on occasions for that purpose. The Church House was also used as a village school as early as 1620, although that does not seem to have lasted for more than 30 years or so.

One of the ways in which Charles II sought to raise money after the Restoration of the monarchy in 1660 was through the imposition of a new tax levied according to the number of fireplaces a dwelling possessed. This was thought to be an accurate way to assess tax liability since hearths or chimneys, being stationary, were easier to count than people. The new tax was dubbed the Hearth Tax or Chimney Tax and one shilling per hearth was to be paid twice a year. There were, however, a number of exemptions for those who were unable to afford such payments, including anyone already assessed as being unable to afford Church or Poor rates, those living in property with an annual rental value of less than £1, and those with assets worth less than £10. All householders were to be listed, including the exemptions. In Langford Budville, Hearth Tax exemption certificates were granted in 1671 to 51 householders. Given that the Lay Subsidy Rolls only 30 years earlier (see The Rich…above), listed 77 properties upon which taxes were imposed, one might surmise that the total number of households in the parish at the time was probably somewhere around 130 (77 + 51 = 128). This ties in quite well with the Protestation Return of 1641 (Civil War, above) where there were 141 adult males listed, although some of these would certainly be sharing a family dwelling. Whatever the precise figures may have been, it would indicate that a high proportion – perhaps over a third – of the population of the parish may have been very poor indeed, albeit not quite destitute.

d) The 18th Century

By the 18th century maps began to make their appearance and we can start to see the village, or at least elements of it, as it was then. Below is a copy of an 18th century map of the Archdeacon of Taunton's fields in the village of Langford Budville (he also had extensive holdings to the west of Langford Heathfield).

Map of Archdeacon's lands.

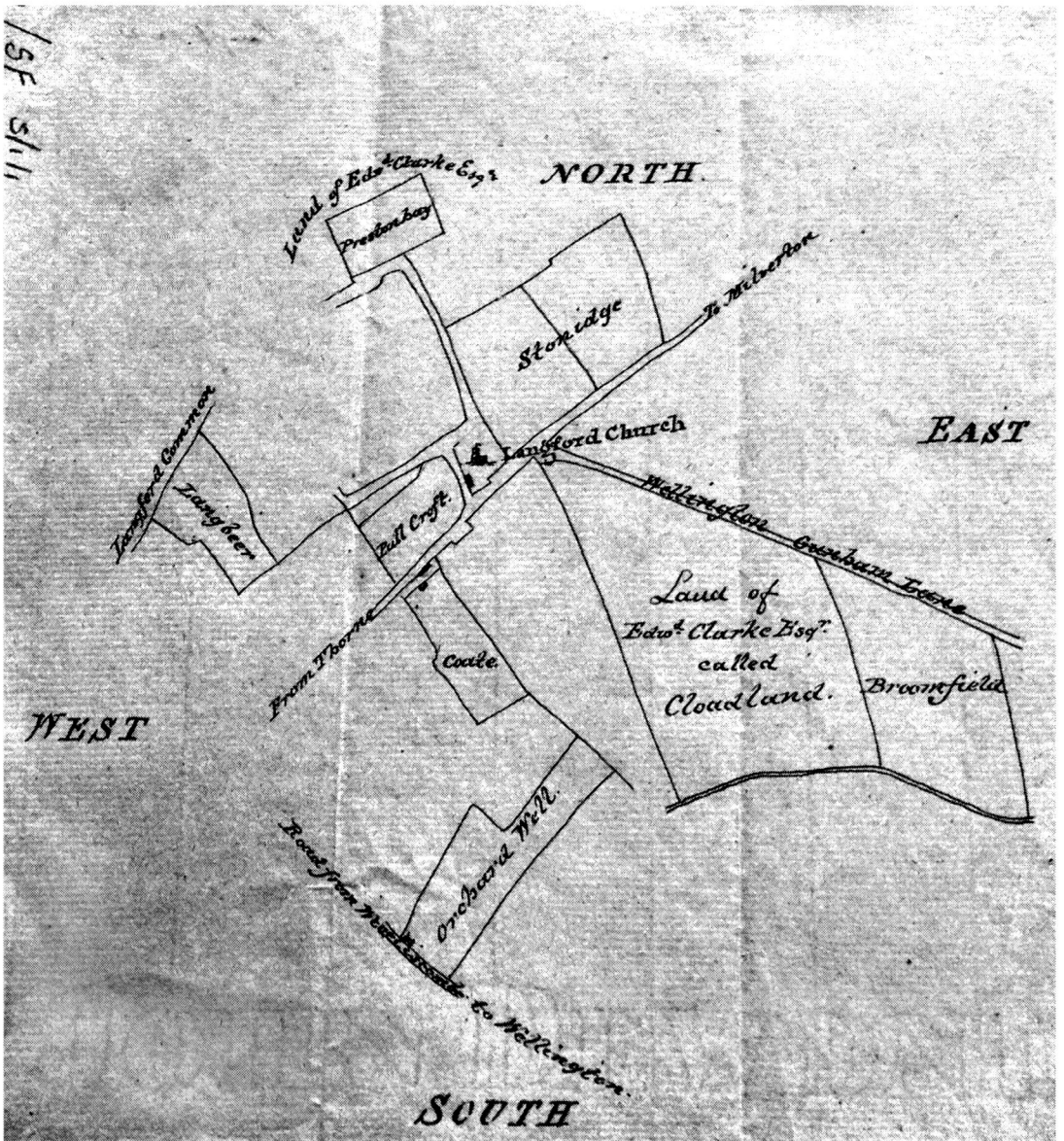

On the east is Langbeare (Saxon – long wood), opposite the Common and not far up the Wiveliscombe road from the Triangle. Prestonhay to the north is opposite Butts Cottages and Stonidge is the plot on the left just past the Church, heading for Langford Gate. Pull Croft is the plot upon which was built Swifts and the other houses bordering the road through the village behind Swifts. Coate is almost certainly the origin of 'Courtlands', which became part of Courtlands Farm and subsequently the modern close of Courtlands. Orchard Well to the south can still be seen on today's Ordnance Survey map with the same field boundaries as in the 18th century (although it is not still called Orchard Well) as can many other old fields. Gunham Lane is now known as Langford Lane, leading down to Gundenham and thence on to Wellington. It would appear that the Archdeacon owned Broomfield to the south of Gunham Lane but that the adjoining field, Cloadland, belonged to Edward Clarke of Chipley – by then probably the most important landowner in the parish.

The Gentry

The Clarkes had arrived at Chipley Park in 1652, Edward Clarke having married into the family of the previous owners (Warres/Lottishams). His great-grandson, also called Edward, was at Chipley Park from 1717 to 1796. In 1756 the Manor of Langford Budville came up for sale at auction. Edward Clarke was keen to acquire it, apparently in part to ensure the undisturbed continuation of his hunting sport, and also to frustrate a rival bidder, William Sanford of Nynehead. The auction took place at the White Hart in Wellington. It appears that there was little love lost between the two principal bidders and Clarke was determined to succeed at almost any cost. His cause was apparently a popular one with the other tenants and the Sanfords, who were already landowners within the parish of Langford Budville, seem to have been viewed as potentially harsh landlords. Clarke in fact received financial support to assist his bid, which was in the event successful.

There were other wealthy residents in the village at about this time, including the Sydenhams, Ritherdons (Langford Court), Havilands (Gundenham) and Webbers (Stancombe). We noted earlier that the Havilands had bought Gundenham back in 1687. They remained there until 1827 and another branch of the Haviland family was at Wellisford. It would appear from the numerous deeds extant from this time that the Ritherdons, Havilands and Webbers not infrequently formed marriage alliances which helped to keep their extensive land holdings intact.

The Working Population

Most of the village would, like their forefathers, have depended on the land for their living, as was confirmed in a 1704 census of the parish of Langford Budville showing the occupations of heads of household. The total population of the parish (obviously larger than the village alone) at the time was in excess of 400.

Gentry, ie annual income of at least £50 per annum: 9
Comer[1] (clerk),   Venner,   Baron (x2),   Webber,
Haviland (x2),   Clatworthy,   Ritherdon.

Almsmen or women: 37 [2]

Husbandmen *(ie tenant farmers)*: 27

Millers: 2

Carpenter: 1

Bachelors: 8 [3]

Tailors: 4

Yeoman *(ie land-owning farmer)*: 1

Blacksmiths: 2

Shoemakers: 2

Bricklayer: 1

Poor: 2 [2]

Combers: 3 [4]

Day labourers: 7

Apprentices: 18

Weavers: 3 [4]

Serge maker: 1 [4]

Cooper: 1

Notes

[1] Revd Nicholas Comer is believed to have been Minister of Kittisford around this time.

[2] It would appear that nearly a third of all households in LB parish relied on alms or other charitable support

[3] It is not understood why bachelors appear to have been rated separately

[4] Note the combers, weavers and serge maker, showing that wool production/processing was important

Writing towards the end of the century, Edmund Rack in his Survey of Somerset (1781) says that the total population of the parish was then upwards of 500 and that there were in all 85 houses. That represents an average of nearly six persons per dwelling, so poverty was evidently still endemic.

Despite the prevalence of farming, Rack asserts that in Langford Budville "agriculture seems imperfectly understood"! There were many large orchards of cider apples and the principal crops grown were wheat and barley. Most of the occupations recorded in the census above were probably still to be found in the village and we know that there were in addition by then 2 public houses. Rack notes that there was "a little spinning." The Fox family of Wellington were the users of much of the wool produced (it was known as 'Taunton serge') and in 1772 they formally founded the famous Fox Brothers company, to which some Langford Budville residents may even in these early days have travelled for work. Rack also records the existence of several stone quarries; the traces of some of these may be seen on the southern end of Langford Heathfield and beyond. There have been other quarries too, for example behind Croxhall, although whether any of these were the quarries to which Rack refers is not known.

Old lime kiln near Langford Heathfield.

Another new occupation introduced in the 18th century was that of turnpike keeper, although this was not a full-time job. The Wiveliscombe Turnpike Trust was established by act of Parliament in 1786 and, like other trusts of its kind, gave local people the opportunity to raise funds for the repair and upkeep of roads, which they could repay through tolls generally levied on wheeled transport or driven livestock. The road from Milverton to Wellington (now the B3187) was turnpiked at what is still sometimes referred to as Langford Gate, at the junction with the road leading off to Langford Budville, and a toll-house was built on the west corner. Road tolls were unpopular, but they did lead to some necessary improvements to the infrastructure at a time of increasing road use, and the magistrates from time to time issued certificates to vouchsafe that the roads were in good repair.

The Church: some random jottings…

Some of the local gentry mentioned above have special commemorative stones in the Church reflecting their status, but a revisit to the Churchwardens' accounts brings us once more back to the mundane everyday matters of the times:

> 1718
>   *Paid George Way half a year for looking*
>   *after the bells and keeping the dogs out of Church*   *5s 6d*
>   *Gave the ringers for King's Coronation Day*   *4s 0d*
> 1720
>   *Gave the ringers for the 5th of November*   *8s 0d*
> 1753
>   *Paid Daniel Bridges for washing the surplice*
>   *and linen about the Church*   *7s 3d*
> 1761
>   *Paid Bennett for teaching the singers*   *£1 17s 6d*

In addition to the singers, there was an orchestra, probably of stringed   instruments

> 1772
>   *Paid John Bridges for the strings for the bass*   *16s 0d*

…and more of the customary slaughter of pests

> 1790
>   *Paid for killing 66 Jays, one Badger and a Hedgehog*   *7s 0d*

A rather disturbing event appertaining to religious matters occurred in Langford Budville in 1740 when the Minister of an Independent Chapel in Wellington, a Mr Darracott, came to Langford Budville, "once a place of great rowdyism", to preach. The locals turned up wielding clubs, swearing and threatening to belabour the Minister if he should attempt to preach. Although the Minister asserted that the house he was visiting was registered for dissenting worship (under the requirements of the Toleration Act of 1698), the leader of the mob retorted that he did not care about the law and the preacher was forced to withdraw. Presumably the local populace were objecting to any deviation from the Anglican tradition, but it seems ironic that this should happen in an area which not many years before was a hotbed of non-conformism.

Another Church anecdote from 18th century Langford Budville concerns the elderly resident who nodded off during a service and started dreaming about cock-fighting, a popular sport of the time. In the middle of his reverie he suddenly yelled out "A shilling on the Red Cock!" to the consternation and, no doubt, amusement of all around him; from henceforth he was always known as The Red Cock.

The base of the cross in the churchyard.

Mention was made above of Edmund Rack's 1781 Survey of Somerset. He records that there was an old stone cross with three rows of steps and a pillar, the top broken off, in the road near one of the two public houses in the village. The most likely location for this would be outside the New Inn, where now stands Old Post (see Public Houses in the chapter on Notable Buildings). From his description it does sound as though he may have been referring to the same base of a cross that now stands in the graveyard outside the south door of the Church.

...and some other unorthodox beliefs!

For much of our history, belief in witchcraft has been common, particularly among country folk. It was once alleged that a (male) witch living in the village kept toads in pots all over his house. If ever he were crossed, he would take a toad, utter a spell and kill it. He would then, it was said, remove its heart, stick it full of pins and hang it up in his chimney with a curse on the offender. In another tale, the landlord of a public house rebuked a witch known locally as Old Maria for taking sticks from his hedge. She cursed him, as a result of which all his livestock died and he met with bad luck for the rest of his life. (Given the reference to livestock this sounds very much like what is now called The Martlet, which once had farmland attached – so landlord beware!)

The village on the map

It was said earlier that the 18th century gave us the opportunity to see Langford Budville in maps of the area, and below is a copy of part of Day and Masters 1782 map of Somerset.

Note that the layout of the village is essentially unchanged today. One should perhaps be cautious in assuming the accuracy of the positioning of individual dwellings, but presumably the draftsman was basing his work on evidence of some sort.

Day and Masters map 1782.

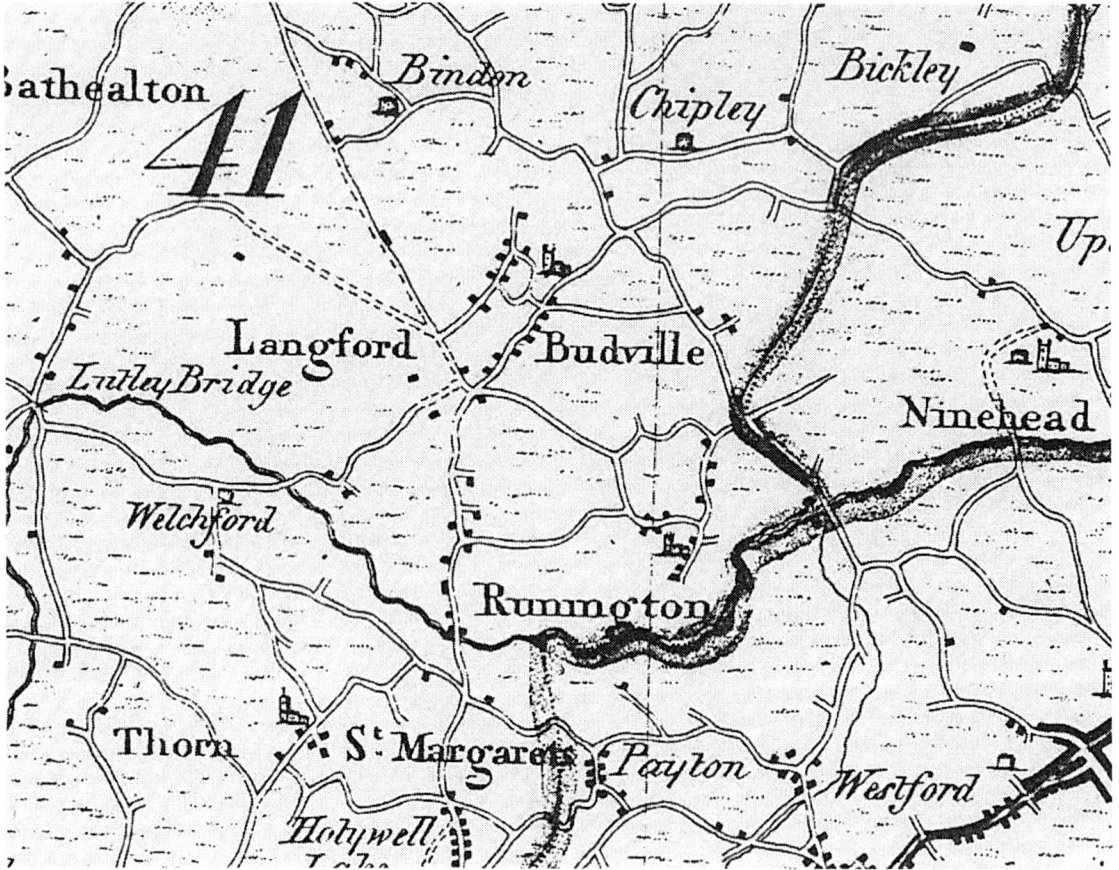

e) The 19th Century – a walk around the village in Victorian times

The maps that follow are from an Ordnance Survey map of 1889. It should be borne in mind that the overwhelming majority of properties in the village were owned by the Sanford family as part of the Nynehead Estate.

We shall start at the top of the village, by St Peter's Church. The Church itself has stood above the village for hundreds of years and its history has been well documented by Mark McDermott elsewhere in this book. The surrounding buildings, however, have changed significantly since Victorian times.

The Church and surroundings (Map 1)

In Map 1 the most obvious change is the absence today of the line of buildings immediately to the south-west of the Church, apart from Hill View at the north end of the row. The four cottages in the middle of the row were at one time called Poor House Cottages and, as the name implies, they had seen service as a refuge and/or house of correction for the destitute of the village. Probably of 16th century origin they, or part of them, had in the distant past been used as a schoolhouse (briefly) and

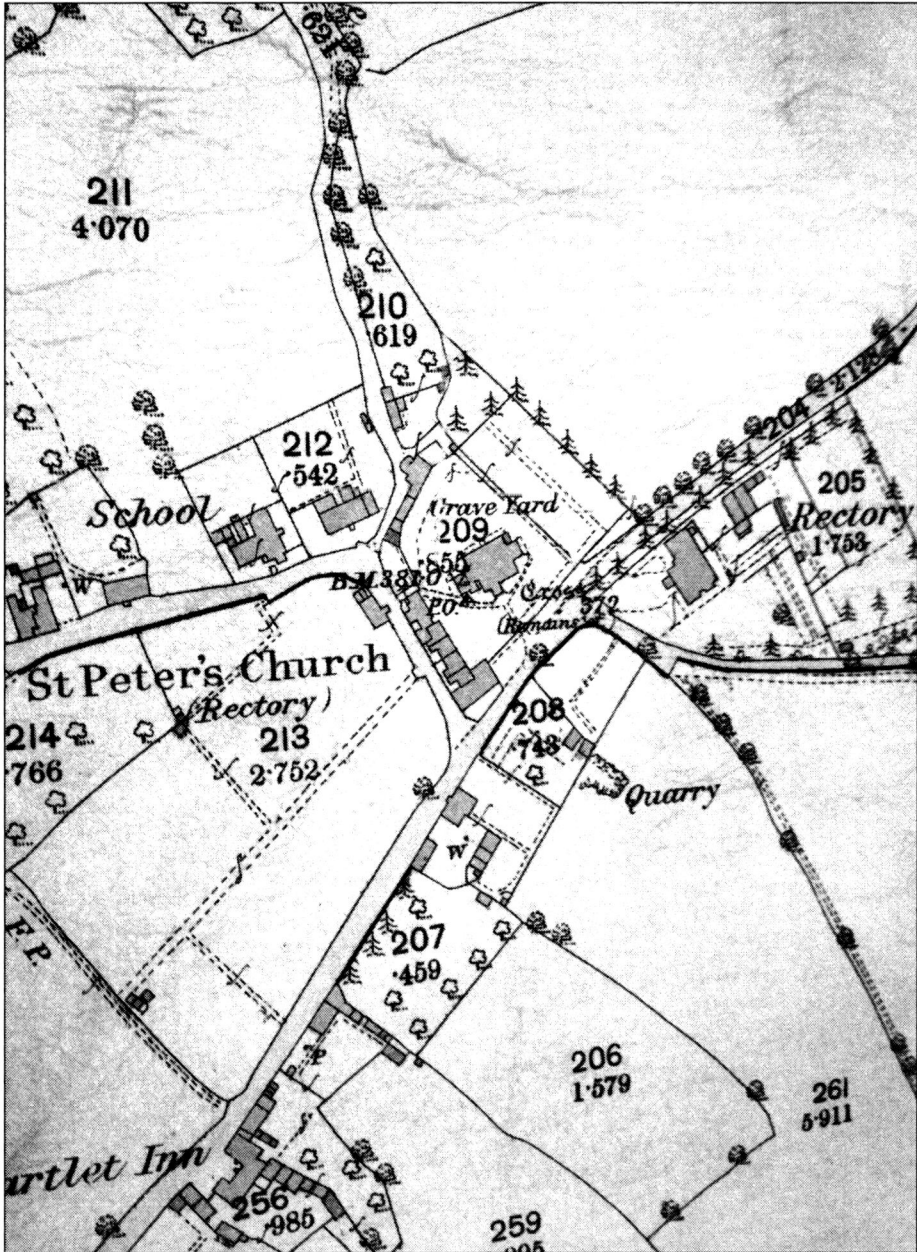

Map 1

the Church House. Following the Poor Law Amendment Act of 1834 it would appear that they were conveyed to the Wellington Union, which took over responsibility for administration of the Poor Law, probably as consideration for the village's contribution to the building of the Union premises in Wellington. However, in 1837 they were sold into private hands and purchased by William Webber, one of the village's blacksmiths. By 1861, the larger property set at right angles on the southern end of the row, facing out across the Tone Valley, was known as Prospect Cottage. Its occupant was John Croxall, a retired butler – originally from Stepney but more recently in service in Wiltshire – a somewhat surprising resident of the village. In 1881 the census described the cottages as Poor House Cottages and Croxall's abode was now called Poor House Villa, something of an oxymoron. After that, the row of houses was renamed Prospect Cottages, with Poor House Villa becoming Prospect House. In 1901 William Comley, Clerk of Works to Col. Sanford of Nynehead Estate, was living in Prospect House. Note that at the time this map was produced (1889) the present Hill View was occupied by the sub-postmaster Joseph Winter, as indicated by the abbreviation P.O. on the map, the village post office having moved across from its previous location in Higher Ritherdons, near Langford Court. Hill View seems to have been distinguished from Poor House Cottages (in the 1881 census it was listed as Crocker's Cottages) and was perhaps never part of the same structure.

The old pencil drawing below from 1855, believed to have been done by Henry Jones, a gardener at Langford Court, shows a view of the Church and surrounding buildings viewed across Peter's Mead, perhaps from a vantage point in Rose Cottages or further round towards Langford Court. The north aisle of the Church has not yet been added (it was built in 1866). The perspective may not be perfect, making it difficult to identify positively all the individual buildings, but the tall, thatched buildings at the back are the only known illustration we have of the old Poor House.

The demise of these properties was one of the more dramatic events in Edwardian Langford Budville. In 1908 the four buildings on the south end of the row – the tall cottages in the sketch above – caught alight. The properties were gutted and much furniture was destroyed. The Fire Brigade arrived from Wellington but were unable to do much to quench the flames as there was no immediately accessible water supply. The buildings were insured by their owner, Col. Sanford of Nynehead, but the possessions of some of the occupants were not and the Vicar, Rev C. H. Luxton, set up a fund for donations to assist them. Hill View is now the only visible trace of these venerable old habitations.

Referring to Map 1 again, there was another property across the road from Hill View. That may perhaps have been the location of the grocer's shop run by the Rugg family in this part of the village and perhaps, earlier, Robert Shattock's butcher's shop, but that has also now gone and has since been replaced by the modern Swifts development. Looking into the top of Butts Lane, the narrow building on the right is still there as Munslow House. Moving west down the road we pass the Old Vicarage, which after the building of Springwood in about 1865 became two cottages for working families; the School, built in 1861 on part of the vicar's glebe land; and then we reach a group of buildings that were once Cload Cottages. The first of these remains as Brockney House, but the others have been demolished and replaced with modern properties. It is believed that in the 1840s William Webber, one of the village's three blacksmiths at that time, had his smithy and foundry here at Cloads.

Coming back up to the Church, to the east is the old Rectory, Springwood, built around 1865, and behind it Coneybeare, named after the plot of land on which it was built. According to the 1843 tithe map, Springwood is on the site of some earlier cottages, owned by John Rugg of Lower Chipley. (This appears to be confirmed by some even older, though less detailed, maps.) Most of the land to the east and north-east of the Church was considered to be part of Lower Chipley and was farmed by John Rugg. Note that Langford Lane is shown as a proper highway, the direct route to Wellington.

Across the road to the south of the Church there appears to be no dwelling but there are two small buildings at the back of a field, perhaps at one time relevant to the quarry. The plot of land between the quarry and the road was called Quarry Close, and in 1874 part of Quarry Close was conveyed by John Gidley (bailiff for the Nynehead Estate) and the aforementioned John Croxall to W. A. Sanford for the purpose of a new house with coach house and stables. The house that was later built here is named Croxhall and it is almost certainly named after John Croxall.

Moving down the road in the direction of Holywell Lake we come to what are now called Old Post and St Peter's Cottage. There was a well behind them and, behind the well, a longer, narrow building, which is still there. Old Post was once a public house named the New Inn but, as the name suggests, soon after this map was prepared, it became another site for the village Post Office run by John Stephens, carpenter, and his wife Mary.

Courtlands to Three Ashes (Map 2)

In Map 2 we continue down the road having passed St Peter's Cottage and come to Courtlands, although it was not known by that name, which is probably a derivative of its much older name of Coat Cottage, standing on a plot called Coatlands. Earlier in the 19th century this premises was a bakery, but by 1851 it was occupied by a mason called

Henry Crocker and later by his son, also named Henry and also a mason. When the son took over, Crocker senior moved up to a cottage near the Church – quite possibly what is today Hill View, which would explain the later description of Crocker's Cottages, see above. In 1881 the mason's house at Coat is referred to as Thomas's (we do not know why) and Henry Crocker Jnr's wife Ann ran a grocery store there. Henry Jnr seems to have retired later to help run the shop. Next to Coat, or Courtlands, is The Martlet about which more is written under the section on Public Houses. The extensive array of outbuildings around the Martlet, then called the Rose and Crown (or simply The Crown) is indicative of the fact that it once had a smallholding attached to it and was run by a farmer.

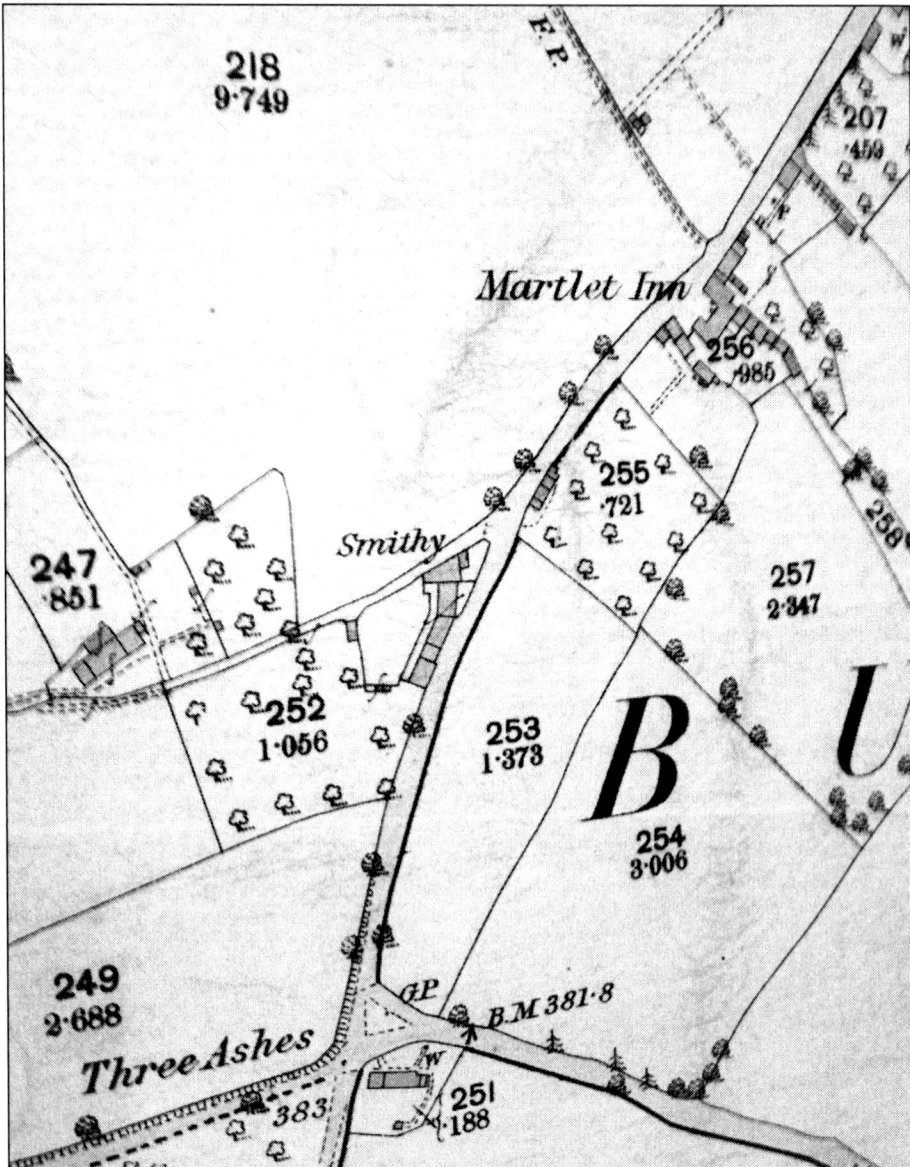

Map 2

There were no more dwellings down the road from the Crown (Martlet) before the smithy on the other side of the road. Through the 19th century this was occupied by a succession of blacksmiths – John Bridges, William Cross (whose wife Eliza was at one time a schoolmistress) and Albert Stone. When William Cross retired in the 1870s he and his wife continued to live in a part of the premises called Babbs Cottage, while Albert Stone took over running the blacksmith's shop. Up the little lane from the smithy were two labourers' cottages called Austin Cottages (they were at one time owned by Elizabeth Austin), later renamed Keeper's Cottages. These have long since been built over by newer properties.

Moving on down to Three Ashes, there was a pair of cottages on the south side of the crossroads, where the modern houses Coppins and The Wedge now stand. These were believed to be referred to as Crossways Cottages and generally housed farm workers. The present cottages along the south side of the road before reaching Three Ashes were not built until about 1907.

Ritherdons and Rose Cottages (Map 3)

Referring to Map 3 (next page) Langford Court (Ritherdons) is dealt with at greater length in this book under the chapter on Notable Buildings. In the 19th century it was a farm forming part of the Nynehead Estate with surrounding meadows, orchards, pasture, arable land and cottages. The building to the west of Ritherdons on the north side of the road was an old thatched cottage called Higher Ritherdons which was part of the farm demesne. This was in the mid-19th century occupied by Robert Gamlin and his wife Ann. The Gamlins farmed 57 acres from Higher Ritherdons in 1861 (while the Curate of Langford Budville, Rev Waldrond, occupied Ritherdons itself) but later Robert had a tailoring business and he and his wife ran the village Post Office at the house. The more recent history of Higher Ritherdons is told by Robert Hayes in the chapter 'Boyhood Memories.' Across the road from Higher Ritherdons there were farm buildings and another cottage.

Coming back round into the village in a south easterly direction there were no further houses until what is now called Rose Cottages. This row of five (or possibly six) dwellings was once called Bowerings Place. The reason for this is unknown but there was a Bowering family living in Langford Budville in the late 18th and early 19th centuries, so there may have been some connection here. They were generally inhabited by agricultural labourers and workers for the wool factory in Wellington, although schoolmistress Elizabeth (Betsy) Blackmore lived there in the 1880s and 1890s. One part of Bowerings occupied by Henry Smith and his family was used from at least as early as 1891 as the village Reading Room. Perhaps this was at the suggestion of Miss Blackmore; at any event it shows an example in Langford Budville of the Victorian virtue of self-improvement.

Finally, we arrive back at Cloads Cottages which we first reached coming from the other direction, so we will now turn around and retrace our steps past Bowerings and turn right on the bend alongside Ritherdons.

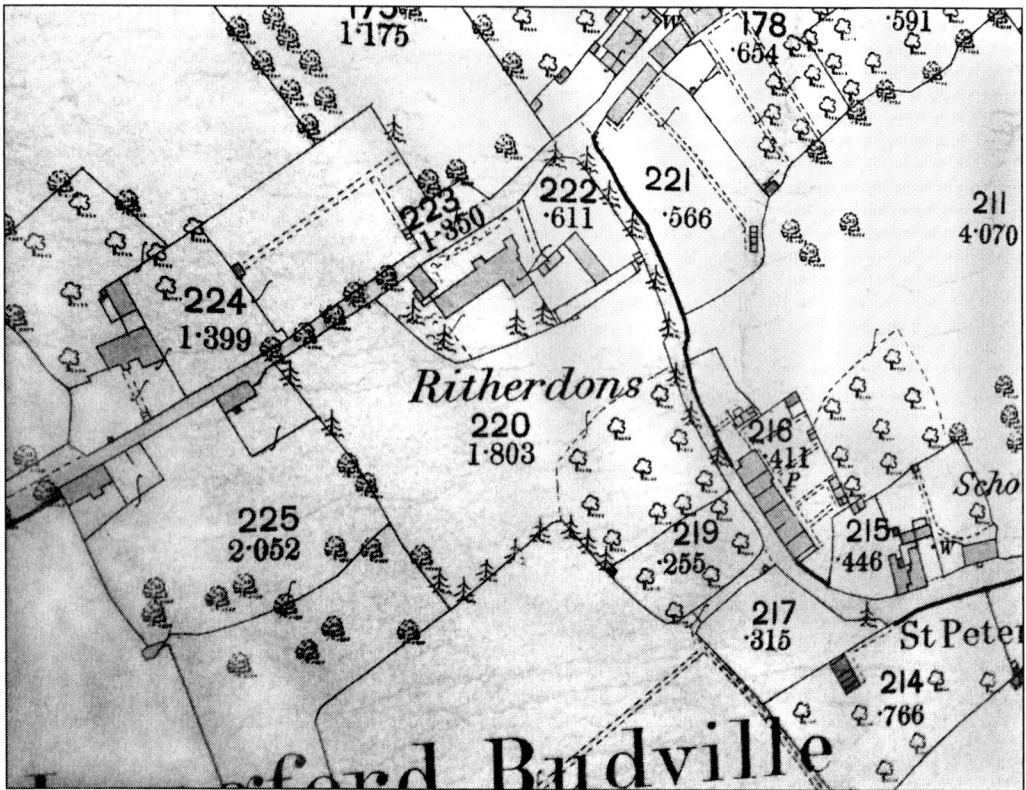

Map 3

Ritherdons to Butts Lane (Map 4)

In Map 4, lining the road on both sides towards the turning into Cholwell Lane were about a dozen cottages, mostly originally with gardens and probably mostly labourers' cottages. The first adjoining two buildings on south side of the road appear to be today's Sunnyview and Sunnyside Cottage. They may have been the Woods Cottages (formerly Crosse Cottages) that appear towards the end of the 19th century censuses, in one of which dwelt a thatcher and his family. However, at the time of the 1843 tithe map it appears that only Sunnyview had been built and there was also a small cottage right on the corner of the road up from Bowerings. As can be seen from the map above, Sunnyside Cottage had been added by 1889 and the corner cottage had vanished. Soon afterwards Chy-an-Mor was erected on the corner plot, adjacent to Sunnyview.

Continuing along the road, the next two cottages, one of which housed a shop, have been demolished and rebuilt in the 20th century as 1 and 2 Chapel View. The last building on the right was owned and occupied in 1841 by Thomas Delbridge who is described as an inn keeper, so there appears to have been a public house for a while on this spot. These premises (it may have been two cottages) were at one time known as Delbridges, later believed to be Reynolds Cottages. In the 20th century they were to be demolished and the Working Men's Club (also since demolished) was built on part of the land.

On the north side of the road, the first few adjoining cottages were burnt down in 1916 – see Alan Tucker's memoirs in 'Family Connections' – but the next, longer building is still there and, after use as a laundry, towards the end of the 19th century became a Chapel for non-conformist worship, continuing as such until the 1980s. Pilgrim Cottage is the small house abutting the Chapel.

Down the bottom of Cholwell (Chorwell) Lane was the well itself and Cholwell Cottage. There had been a property on this spot for hundreds of years, with an early reference to a proposal to build there in 1594. In Victorian times it seems to have been a home for some of the less well-off inhabitants of the village. In 1841 there were in fact two families living there; George Hutchings, a carpenter, with his wife and children and Fanny Taylor, washerwoman, and her daughter. Subsequent occupiers were generally the families of agricultural labourers until Elizabeth Clements and her children moved in from Keeper's Cottages (near the Old Forge) early in the 1900s. She was still there in 1926 which was presumably not many years before it was finally demolished.

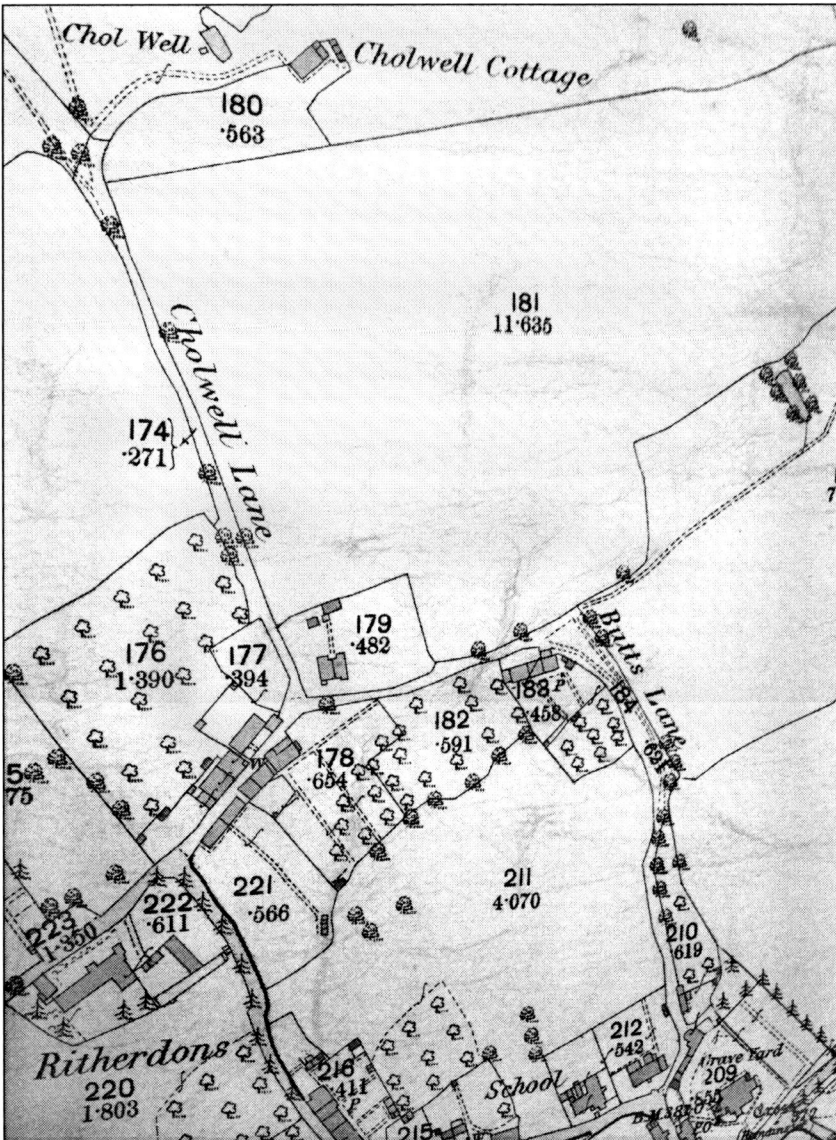

Map 4

Returning back up Cholwell Lane, a building was shown on the 1843 tithe map at the top on the western corner but this had disappeared by the time of the map shown above. There is a modern house there now. On the east side is a pair of cottages known as Shattocks, still occupied today. Shattocks is a very old name indeed; Thomas Shattocke, a weaver, is listed in 2 registers of villagers from 1641 (see section on 17th century) and in 1711 Robert Shattocke and others covenanted to pay Jepp Clarke of Chipley for the right to draw water from a well adjoining the late Thomas Shattocke's land (maybe the well was Chol Well?). A plot of land referred to as Shattocks is also included in a 1716 marriage settlement of the Clarke family of Chipley. In 1800 a lease of Shattocks was granted to Abel Bridges and we know from the 1843 tithe map that Bridges still tenanted the plot on which Shattocks Cottages stand. However, it is likely that the present cottages were built sometime after 1843.

The 20th century buildings now lining the road down towards Butts Lane are not of course part of our tour, but it is interesting to speculate as to the origin of the name Reynolds, which was applied to the three semi-detached properties now situated on the south side of the road. Together with Thomas Shattocke, Robert Reynolds was one of those involved in the agreement to pay Jepp Clarke for use of a well in 1711, so he probably occupied land quite close to Shattocks. Then in 1769 James Reynolds (probably a descendant) conveyed a house and an acre of land in Langford Budville to William Delbridge, a miller from Nynehead. Delbridge or his descendants later moved into Langford Budville. As noted above, in 1843 they owned and occupied a property opposite the top of Cholwell Lane which later appears to have been referred to as Reynolds Cottages and they also owned the adjacent land upon which the modern Reynolds houses were built. So the whole plot of land may have been known as Reynolds after its 18th century owners, Robert and James Reynolds, right up until the present day.

At the bottom of the hill on the corner of Butts Lane are Butts Cottages. These three cottages were generally occupied by labourers' and wool workers' families in the 19th century. For a while they were also known as Young's Cottages, although it is not clear why this name was applied. However, by 1881 one of the houses was being used as a meeting house for religious worship and was the forerunner of the Chapel that was established back up the hill some time after 1893.

The Surrounding Area

Time has not allowed for detailed research into all the outlying property beyond the confines of the village itself, but a look at the 1889 OS map may be of interest.

Bindon and Middle Hill (Map 5)

The outline of the grounds of Bindon House (see chapter on Notable Buildings) remains largely unchanged today. Note the old quarry behind Bindon Farm and the narrow building by the Wiveliscombe road near the end of the drive to Bindon House. This was Heathfield Ford, at one time the Hare and Hounds public house. The terrain was clearly quite wet to judge by the several ponds and the stream with its pump house. The lake to the west of Middle Hill Wood is the now the location of the larger recreational fishing lakes of Middle Hill Farm. Abel Bridges was the tenant farmer at Middle Hill for a number of years in the 19th century.

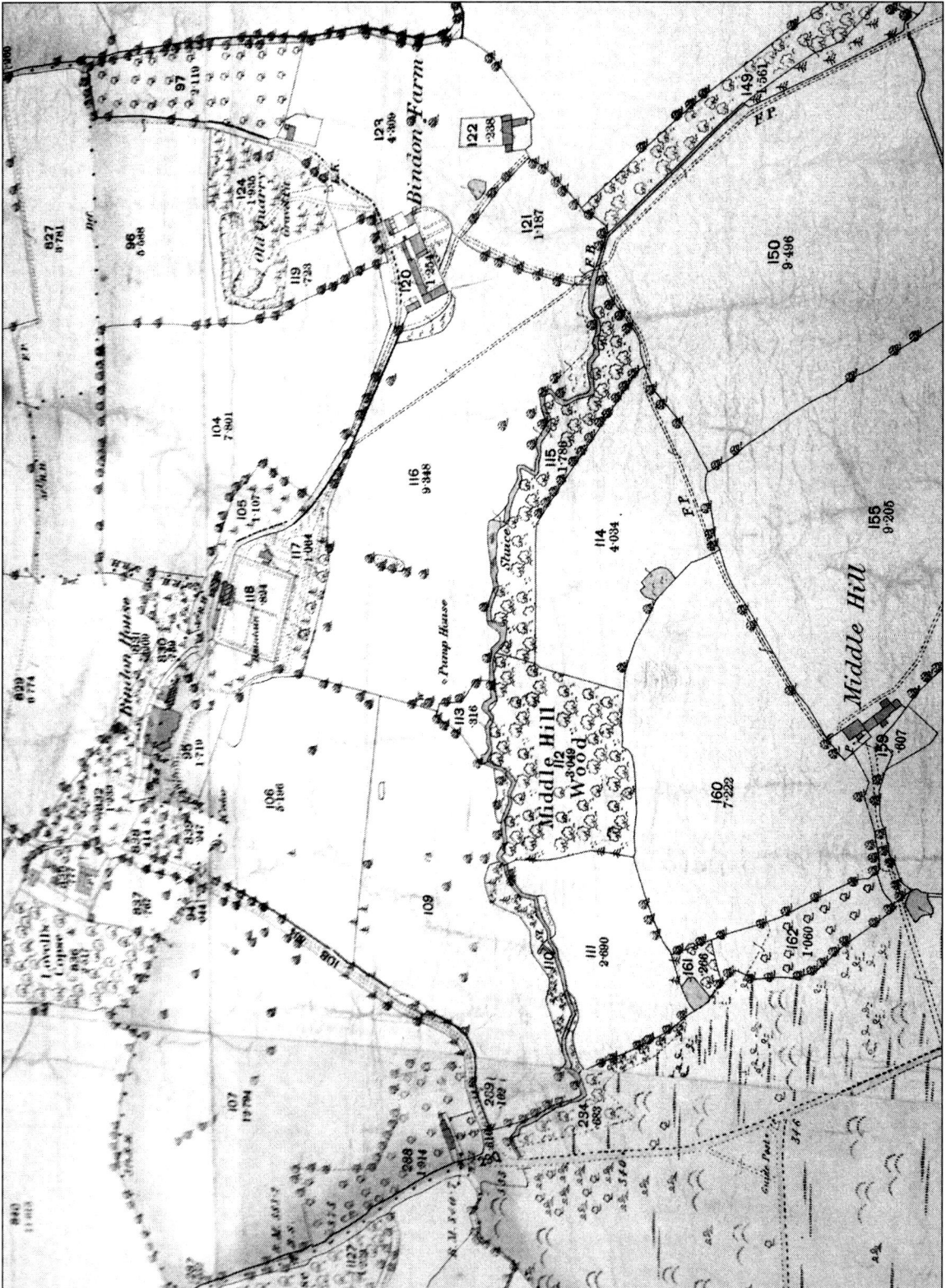

Map 5

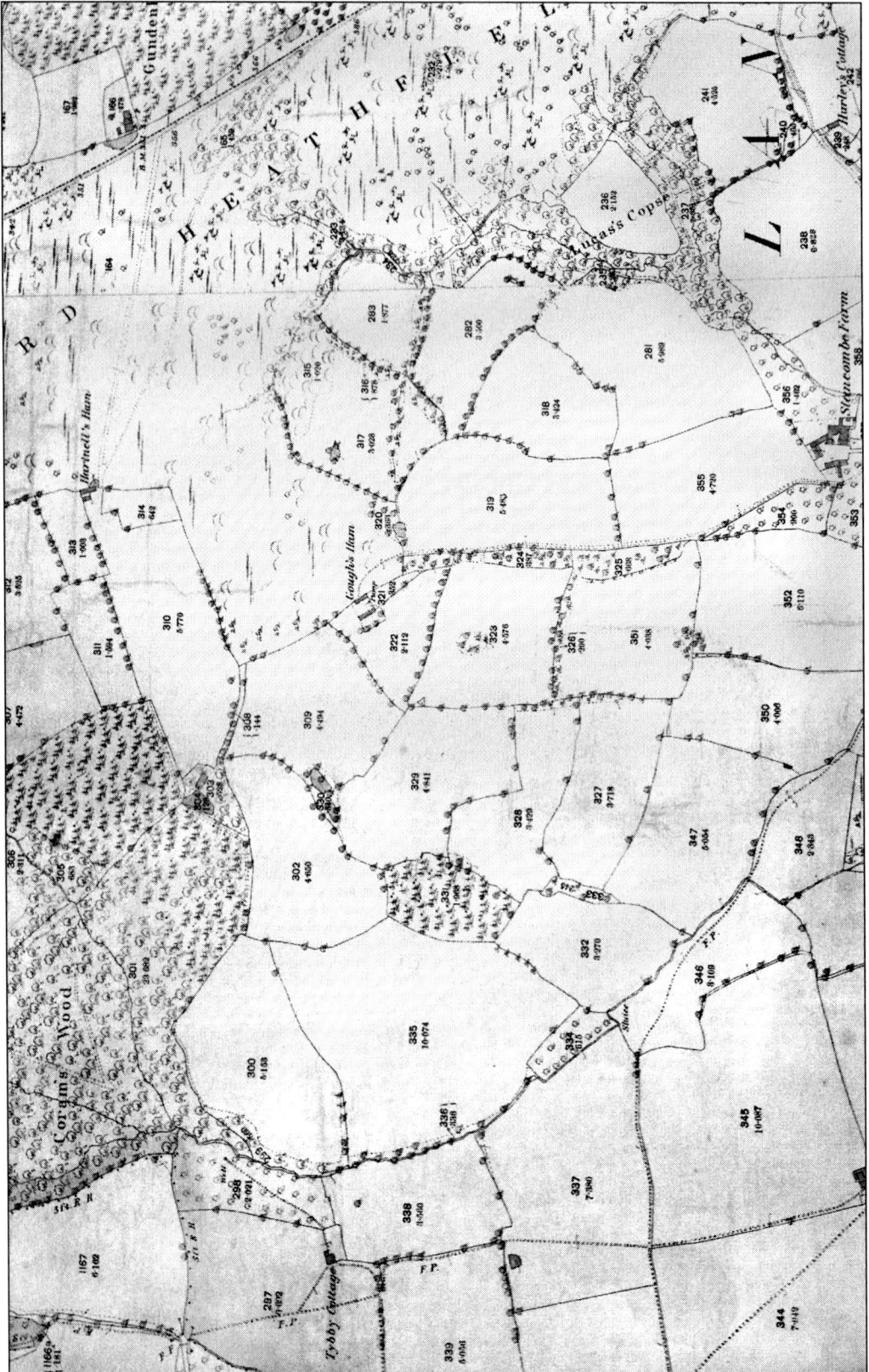

Map 6

Lands to the west of the village (Map 6)

In this area were some habitations of great antiquity, most of which are sadly no longer with us. Tybby Cottage on the western edge has been referred to in earlier sections and the name (Tybhay) goes back hundreds of years, but it was probably abandoned early in the 20th century. Likewise Hartnell's Ham in the north and Gough's Ham in the centre were originally farms built on tracts of land bearing those names which were for centuries part of the Archdeacon of Taunton's estates. Later, they became labourers' cottages but were abandoned many years ago.

Gundenham (Map 7)

As already noted, Gundenham, again with various spellings, is a very old name in Langford Budville. (See the chapter on Notable Buildings for a brief history.) The 1889 map is fairly easily related to the current configuration. At the beginning of the 19th century Gundenham was farmed by the Rugg family, as tenants first of Edward Clarke and then of John Nurton of the Chipley Estates. John Rugg was raised there by his parents and took charge of the farm at the age of 19 or 20, probably after the death of his father. He was appointed Estate Bailiff under Nurton. In 1829 Edward Sanford inherited the Chipley Estates but remained at the family seat in Nynehead. One of his early actions seems to have been to dispossess the tenant of Lower Chipley Farm, Charles Surrage, in 1831 apparently for non-payment of rent. Immediately after this, John Rugg took over at Lower Chipley while John Bailey moved into Gundenham. It is perhaps worth mentioning that the redoubtable John Rugg was still living in Chipley in 1861 – though not still farming – at the age of 92! There were a succession of tenant farmers at Gundenham in Victorian times following John Bailey. Charles Rowsell was there for at least 25 years until the late 1870s. Then came William Salway and around the turn of the century Thomas Ewens Walters. One of the striking features of Gundenham throughout the 19th century

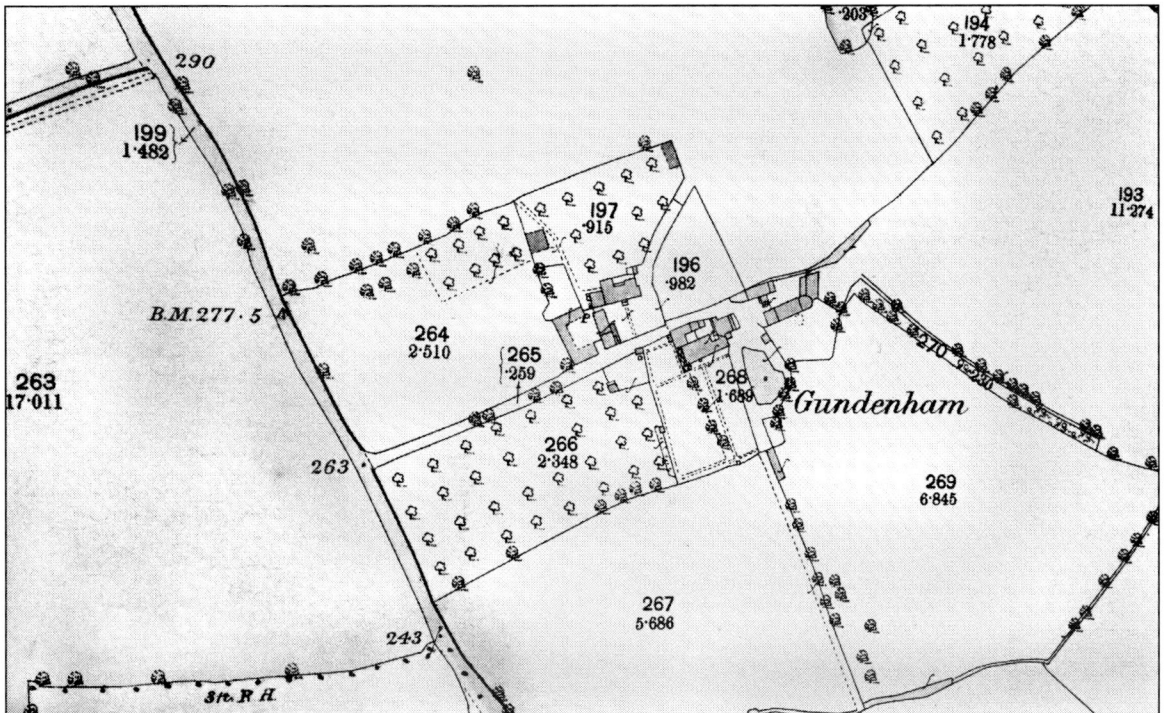

Map 7

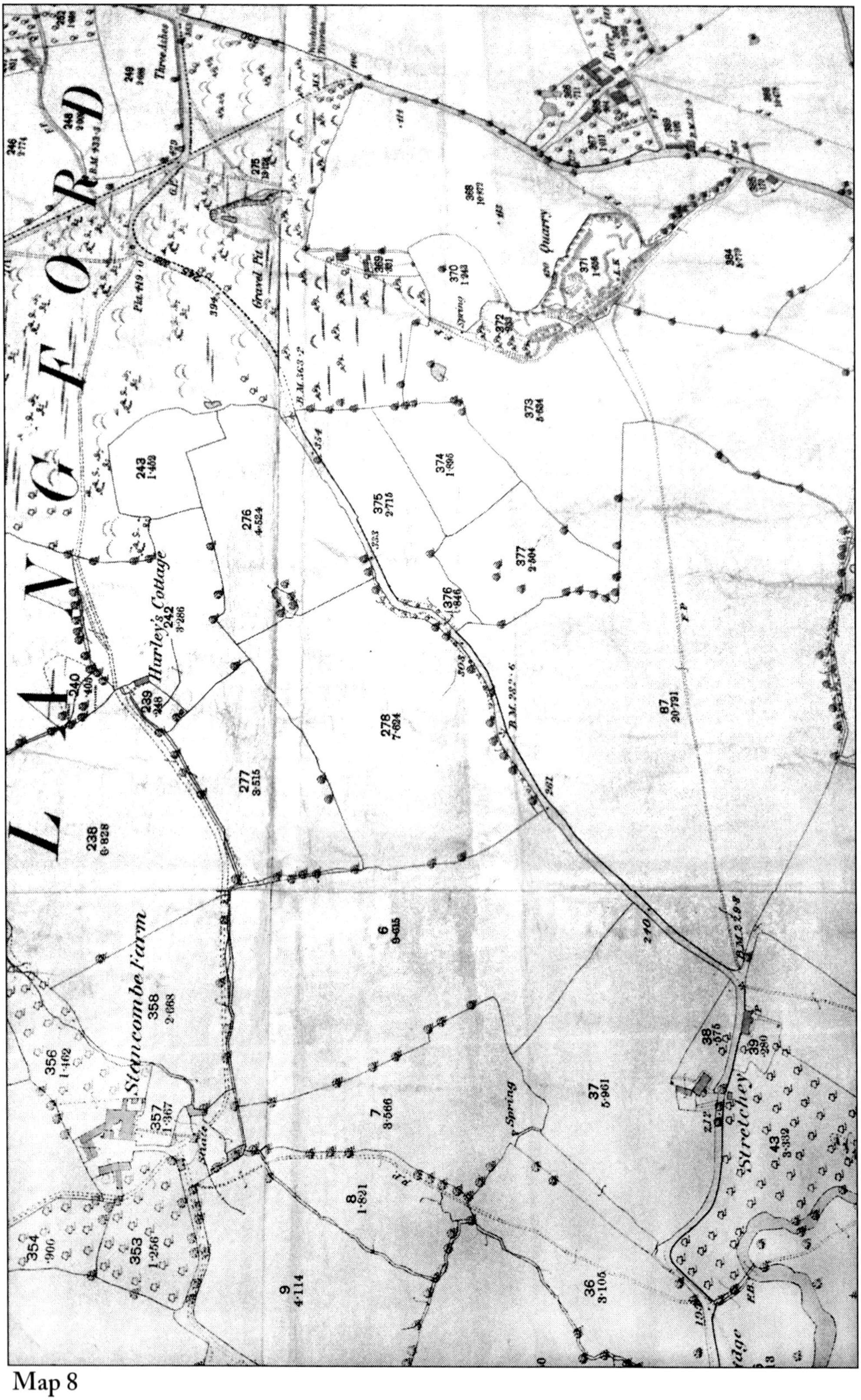

Map 8

and beyond was the number of persons living in and around the farm, reflecting both the larger families of the times and the need for labour on the land. In addition to the farmhouse there were three cottages occupied by farm labourers and their families; by 1881 this had grown to 4 cottages. There were generally in excess of 20 persons, including children, living in the farm property – in fact by 1911 this had reached 29. While the men worked on the land, their wives and elder daughters sometimes went to work in the wool factories in Wellington. The farmers' families at Gundenham usually employed a live-in servant; Thomas E. Walters had two, even though he, his wife and son-in-law were the only occupants of the farmhouse.

The south west (Map 8)

Stancombe Farm, as a farm location, is again of great age with records going back to the 14th century. Stancombe seems always to have remained a place of some standing and remains inhabited today. On the other hand Hurley's Cottage (centre north), a home for farm workers, has long since disappeared. Another very old location mentioned earlier is Stretchey, in the south west corner on the road from Langford Budville to Wellisford. This, together with Stroudshayes (probably the same root) another nearby cottage, also go back to the 14th century but have now vanished. Also of interest is what is now called Paradise Cottage, un-named on this map but located just below the gravel pit (now a children's cycle ramp) on the east of the map. Paradise Cottage was known as Stone's Cottage(s) and was occupied, perhaps built, by the Stone family in the early part of the 19th century. Later in Victorian times it was occupied by the Pike family and at one time housed two families.

Harpford to Bere (Map 9)

Harpford Farm and Mill were always substantial enterprises within the parish, although a detailed history is outside the scope of this book. As may be seen from map 9, overleaf, the mill was no longer in operation by 1889. Up the road towards the village lies Ramsey Farm, another farmstead recorded way back in the early 14th century. One of the buildings next to the farm has been known for years as Cobbetts (or Cobbs) Castle. The evidence of some old deeds suggests that this may be a derivation from Coppice (or Copse) Castle, presumably with reference to some nearby woodland, though where the description 'Castle' comes from is unknown. Continuing towards Bere (Beer) Farm was a small labourer's cottage on the left called variously Stuckey Pitts or Stockey Pit. The origin of the name is unknown, but may have been an allusion to the nearby quarry. Finally we arrive at Bere Farm, the general layout of which seems much as it is today. A few hundred years ago, Bere (Beer or Beare, the spelling varies) comprised 2 tenements, Higher and Lower Bere, perhaps one on either side of the highway. In any event, they have long been combined and formed a substantial farm throughout Victorian times.

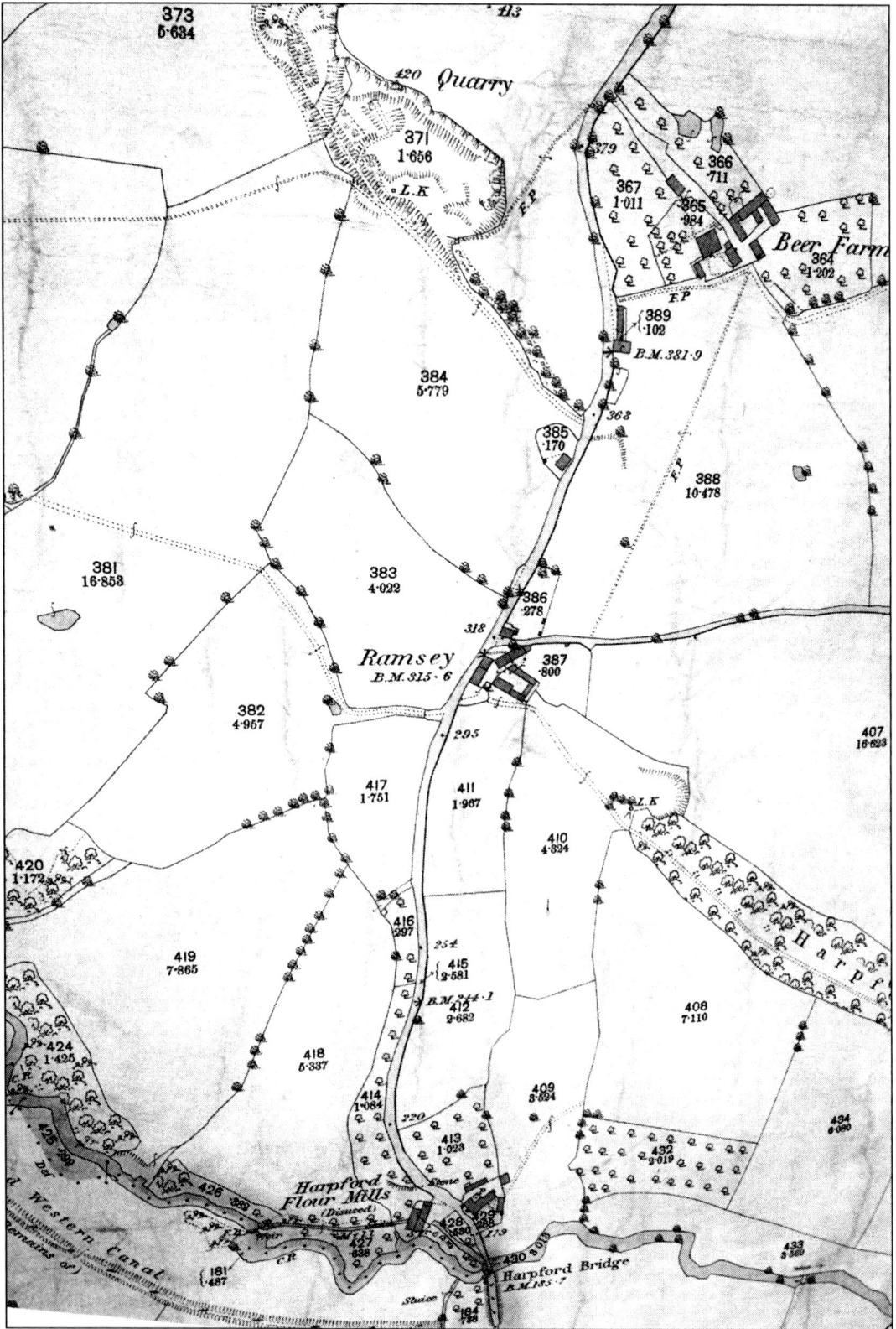

Map 9

Chapter 2 – **FIRST WORLD WAR**
Alan Tucker

Seventy names are listed on the Roll of Honour at the back of St Peter's Church and I have discovered a further thirteen that could have been included. It is not clear upon what basis someone compiled the roll of those who served and wrote it up in copperplate handwriting. Fifty-seven of the overall total did have connections with Langford Budville links either at the time of the war, before the war, or were born in the village.

The names listed on the roll reflect the three services – army, navy and air force but also include three nurses. They include men who saw active service, others who joined late in the war and did not leave England and those whose contribution was behind the lines or at home. Seven men died in the war and one afterwards and are listed on the separate memorial plaque in the church. However, a further five deaths can be identified – three during the war and two afterwards. For the army, twelve officers are represented and, with other men, were drawn from the pre-war regulars who became the Old Contemptibles, as well as the Territorials, Kitchener volunteers and conscripts. Some men were career soldiers who had joined the army before 1914 or had also joined the navy; some had served as Territorials before 1914. There were infantry privates and NCOs, gunners, drivers and sappers.

Forty-four men and one of the nurses saw active service abroad in a variety of theatres of war. Some men served on the Western Front in France and Belgium but other places also feature – India, Gallipoli, Egypt, Palestine, Salonika and Mesopotamia. Three of the men were very early arrivals at the front – John Keates and Frederick Westcott both arrived in France on August 21 1914 with the regulars of the 1/Somerset Light Infantry. Around the same time Nigel Kennedy Worthington, an officer in the 3/Dragoon Guards, did the same.

For one man the war ended before Great War service, as his war was in Northern Russia on the 'White' side of the Russian civil war in 1918-19. This was Private Harold Woodroffe of the 6/Royal Marine Light Infantry who joined up soon after his 18th birthday in 1917. He was a footman so must have worked in one of the large houses. On the Roll there was also a recruiting officer and a trainer. There was a Canadian and an Australian, Private Walter Palmer, a farm hand from Melbourne who joined the 39th Australian battalion in September 1916 and saw service in France. One man served in the Army of Occupation after the war and fourteen, including one nurse, served at home for a variety of reasons – their type of service e.g Army Service Corps, late mobilisation, too young when called up and still in training, the recruiter and the trainer

The wealthier households
The 'big houses' of the area are well represented although it is not always possible to distinguish owners from tenants. Bindon House was the home of Lieutenant Nigel Kennedy Worthington in 1901. He had joined the Dragoon Guards before the war and was in France in 1914; in 1915 he won the Military Cross near Ypres. Major Thomas Reynolds lived there in 1914 and the house and estate were bought by Captain James Hamilton Leigh in 1915. Leigh joined the Queens Own Cameron Highlanders before the war which he spent training recruits with rifles and machine guns.

Lieutenant Reginald Cross was living at Wellisford Manor in 1910 and Captain David Howard Evans in 1914, followed by Captain Anthony Knight sometime afterwards. Cross was in the 2/4th South Lancs when he was killed near Arras on June 7 1918. Evans had served in the Boer War and was with the Dragoon Guards. He served with them, probably at home, during the first part of the war but then became an Assistant Provost Marshall in France and subsequently the Taranto base, Italy. Captain Knight served in the Norfolks and was wounded at Gallipoli in August 1915. In 1916 he was in Egypt but from late 1917 began to suffer boils on the chest which forced him to return to England for a long period of recovery.

Croxhall, opposite the church, was a new house built before the war and was the home of Colonel Loscombe in 1911. Loscombe was already 58 when the war broke out and had joined the army in the late 1880s. He had commanded a battalion of the West India Regiment in Jamaica. For about nine months from September he commanded the 9/South Staffs, a Kitchener New Army unit, but did not take them to France. Afterwards he commanded the 1st Garrison Battalion of the Cheshires in Gibraltar.

Major Paton was at Chipley Park by the end of the war. He was an officer in the Manchester Regiment as early as the 1890s, had retired but came back to command a home depot and work as Assistant Inspector of Recruiting for Southern Command before a second retirement because of ill-health in 1916.

The existence of the dwellings of the wealthy also accounts for servicemen whose occupations had been footmen (2), gardeners (3), a groom and a green-keeper at the golf course on the Common. Farmers, usually their sons, and their workers are well represented as well as those lured by factory employment in the woollen factories at Tonedale in nearby Wellington or at Westford.

Personal connections

James Hayes, the writer's grandfather, was a sapper who joined up in 1916 and served with the 258 Tunnelling Company, Royal Engineers, at Hill 70, north of Lens, and on the Somme after the 1916 battle.

Earlier in the century he had gone to South Wales with two brothers and worked in coal mines which meant that he was a natural recruit into the tunnellers during the war. After 1909 he had been a green-keeper at the golf course on the Common; at the latter he was photographed with his wife and young children late in the war having been transferred to the Labour Corps as a result of ill health caused by underground gas.

His brother, Tom, who worked at Chipley Saw Mill and was the writer's great-uncle, was a regular soldier who had served in India in the Northumberland Fusiliers before the war. His service at the front, early in the war, was cut short by a gunshot wound in July 1915 which probably involved the loss of fingers on the right hand.

Jimmy Hayes - sapper

Langford Heathfield c1917 4th man from left Jimmy Hayes – seated on the logs Mary Ann Hayes his wife with children Ernest, Rene, Vera & Albert.

The Somerset Light Infantry

Unsurprisingly seventeen men had joined the Somerset Light Infantry in a wide range of battalions. One of these was Private Hubert Braddick (another great-uncle), who was killed in the Ypres area on September 3 1917. He had been awarded the Military Medal and is commemorated on the Menin Gate.

Another was Private Henry Clements who was discharged in April 1918 after receiving shrapnel wounds in France. Between the wars he always laid the main wreath at the annual remembrance ceremony at St. Peter's Church, Langford Budville. A variety of other regiments are represented on the list. Nine served in the artillery, and the newly formed Tank Corps and Machine Gun Corps provided three men. Gunner Gilbert Brewer served in the Royal Field Artillery having joined up in November 1914 at the age of 19. He was at the front for over a year when he was discharged wounded in November 1916. Another artilleryman was Driver Frederick Jones who had joined up in 1916 from his home at Poleshill. In October 1916 he went to Salonika where he contracted malaria before the end of the war. Private William Yeo was in the 6th Battalion of the

G v R I

HE whom this scroll commemorates was numbered among those who, at the call of King and Country, left all that was dear to them, endured hardness, faced danger, and finally passed out of the sight of men by the path of duty and self-sacrifice, giving up their own lives that others might live in freedom. Let those who come after see to it that his name be not forgotten.

*Pte. Hubert Charles Braddick, M.M.
1 Somerset Light Inf*

Commendation Certificate

Tank Corps and came from Butts Cottage where he left a wife, Elizabeth, and two sons. Seven had become cavalrymen or served with the Yeomanry. Eight men had joined the Royal Navy or the Royal Marine Light Infantry.

The Nurses

Three nurses were listed, one of whom faced having to deal with the terrible wounds of war in France. This was Alice Edwards of Fursdons Farm. As a Voluntary Aid Detachment nurse throughout she served in war hospitals at Frome, Warminster, Bristol and on the hospital ship, Aquitania. From July 1917 she served in four military hospitals in France at Amiens, Le Treport, Rouen and Boulogne. Her younger sister, Kate, was a Red Cross nurse serving at a war hospital at Exeter.

Decorated for Valour

Four men were medal winners – two won a Military Medal and two a Military Cross. Private George Parnell of Middle Chipley Farm was one of the MM recipients whilst serving with the 6th/Wiltshire Regiment in France in 1918.

Families with multiple combatants

Some families were able to make a greater contribution than others, such as the six Thresher brothers, four Crowcombe brothers, two Ewens sisters and one brother, and eight pairs of brothers – Clements, Hayes, Jones, Keates, Pike, Tarr, Winwood, Chipling and Toogood. The six Thresher brothers were…

   Private Albert, Somerset Light Infantry. Discharged as a result of wounds in June 1918

   Private Harry, also Somerset Light Infantry, was stationed in India throughout the war

   Corporal George also served in the same regiment and died of food poisoning in India on September 2 1916

   Frank served in the Royal Navy

   Private John served in the 2nd Devons and died of wounds on July 13 1916 received on the Somme. He was a pre-war regular who had served at Malta. He was buried in Devizes Road Cemetery, Salisbury

   Private Tom saw active service with the Kings Yorkshire Light Infantry, the Somerset Light Infantry and the Labour Corps

   Private George Toogood from Beer Farm probably saw active service in the Middle East and France in the West Somerset Yeomanry. His brother, Harry, served in the same regiment, including at Gallipoli. Captain Thomas Winwood was killed at his forward observation post in the Battle of Doiran in Salonika on April 28 1917 whilst serving in the 99th Brigade, Royal Field Artillery. He had returned to England at the start of the war from Alberta, Canada, where he was a rancher. He was awarded a posthumous Military Cross and left a wife, Mabel. His younger brother was Captain John Winwood who was a pre-war regular in the Dorsets. In September 1916 he joined the 1st Garrison Battalion of the Devons in Egypt but later came back to England suffering from a duodenal ulcer and did not serve again. He died in Switzerland in 1922.

Alan Tucker attended Langford Budville School from 1954-9. He has a grandfather, James Hayes, and three great-uncles listed on the Roll. The full version of this article can be found on the internet at http://www.hellfirecorner.co.uk/tucker/tuckerroll.htm

The Village at War 1914-18

What must life have been like during the First World War? One can only surmise what deprivation, worry and grief villagers had to bear. Apparently the church was full every Sunday. It is well known that Fox Bros were the main supplier of puttees for the soldiers in the trenches and undoubtedly people living in Langford Budville were employed in their making. It is said they made 13 miles of puttees per week.

REJOICING OVER THE GOOD NEWS

The news that Germany had signed the armistice and the war was practically over, reached Langford before midday on Monday 11th November 1918. The flag was at once hoisted on the Church Tower and two volleys were fired on 3 anvils at the village smithy (Mr. Stone's). It was not long before flags were put out at many private houses and during the afternoon merry peels were rung on the bells of the Church. In the evening the children, their parents and other relatives assembled in the Village Club Room and spent a happy time. Selections were played on Mrs. Till's gramophone, games were indulged in and for a couple of hours there was dancing, the duties of the accompanist being kindly undertaken by Miss Brimblecombe. Every credit is due to those who got up so successful a gathering.

Wellington Weekly News
November 13th 1918

Chapter 3 – SECOND WORLD WAR

"I am speaking to you from the Cabinet room at 10 Downing Street. This morning the British Ambassador in Berlin handed the German Government an official note stating that unless we heard from them by eleven o'clock, that they were prepared at once to withdraw their troops from Poland, a state of war would exist between us. I have to tell you now that no such undertaking has been received, and consequently this country is at war with Germany."

These were the opening words of Prime Minister Neville Chamberlain's wireless broadcast to the nation at 11.15am on Sunday, 3rd September 1939. One wonders how many people in Langford Budville listened to the broadcast that morning on their wireless – at any rate, those who were not in church!

The Home Guard

After the British Expeditionary Force was driven into a tactical withdrawal towards the coast at Dunkirk it was obvious that Hitler was not going to stop at the Channel. People began to express their concern at the state of the nation's defences and demanded an opportunity to be able to defend their homeland. And so on Tuesday 14th May 1940 people tuning in their wireless sets heard an appeal made by Anthony Eden, the secretary of State for War:

"…We want large numbers of such men in Great Britain, who are British subjects, between the ages of 17 and 65, to come forward now and offer their services in order to make assurance doubly sure. The name of the new Force which is now to be raised will be 'The Local Defence Volunteers'. This name describes its duties in three words. It must be understood that this is, so to speak, a spare time job, so there will be no need for any volunteer to abandon his present occupation…"

Over a quarter of a million men volunteered overnight and well over a million by July of that year when the organisation was renamed the Home Guard. Throughout the country, village by village and factory by factory, sections, platoons, companies and battalions were organised to defend against invasions of German paratroops. It is sobering to remember that some of those who volunteered in 1940 had already been through the horrors of the 1st World War and bore the scars, both mental and physical of that conflict only 22yrs before. Some were fresh-faced young men who joined whilst waiting for their call-up. Confusion sometimes occurred when veterans of the 1st World War continued to use their previous wartime rank whilst serving in the Home Guard. Unlike the Regular Army, the Home Guard was a local force based in its own area and it proved impossible to form units of regulation size.

Factories began to work flat out to make up the loss of military hardware sustained at Dunkirk in anticipation of a protracted war and the Home Guard requirements became a low priority. This is when British ingenuity and enterprise came to the fore and weapons were gathered from many sources – even museums! Rifles came from America and from private individuals.

Training was given by WW1 veterans, regular officers and the Home Guard Travelling Wing and so the Home Guard developed into a creditable force of companies and platoons with pre-planned schemes should the enemy invade. They played their part in guarding strategic buildings such as railway goods yards and factories that were turning out vital war supplies.

After June 1944, with the Allies firmly established in Europe, the role of the Home Guard diminished and from September of that year duties were no longer compulsory. Stand Down Parades were held throughout the country in the December.

The most tangible 'monument' to these men are the pill boxes, some of which still remain, where the men of the regular army together with their contemporaries in the Home Guard were prepared to defend their homeland 'to the last round, to the last man'. A special army order was issued to the Home Guard with a message from King George VI on 3rd December 1944:

"History will say that your share in the greatest of all our struggles for freedom was a vitally important one. You have given your service without thought of reward. You have earned in full measure your country's gratitude"

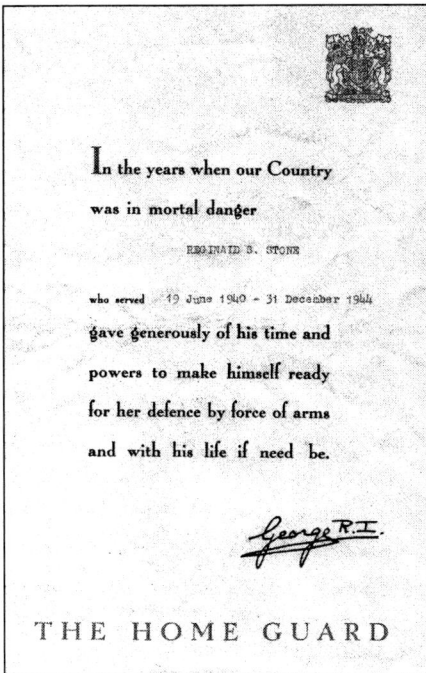

In the years when our Country was in mortal danger

REGINALD S. STONE

who served   19 June 1940 - 31 December 1944

gave generously of his time and powers to make himself ready for her defence by force of arms and with his life if need be.

George R.I.

THE HOME GUARD

Langford Budville Home Guard

2nd Somerset (Taunton) Battalion
Commanding Officer: Colonel Lewin-Harris

'F' (Wellington) Company
Commanding Officer: Major Leo G. 'Pukka' Dawe T.D.
(Art Master Wellington School)
Company Adjutant: Capt. T. Fox
Staff Officer: Capt. O.S. 'Oscar' Hughes
(Junior House Master at Wellington School)
Platoon Commander: Capt. T. Fox

No definitive/accurate list of names has been found – below are those remembered:

John Bradbury, Harold Brewer, Colin Burgess had a 12 bore shot gun,

Bill Cottey, Jim Cottrell had a .22 rifle which his son John still has,

Walter Harris, Reg Stone, Kenneth Toogood.

Platoon headquarters and Mr. Fox's office were in what is still the headquarters of the Somerset Cadet Battalion (The Rifles) ACF, a red brick building on the north side of Mantle St. which still contains a licensed rifle range used periodically by Wellington School CCF, among others. It took Mr Fox twenty minutes at a fast walk to get to this office from Fox's Tonedale Factory.

On one exercise the Langford Budville Platoon were asked to guard the electricity sub station – on the left before the bridge at Tonedale. Captain Fox in true Captain

Mainwaring style donned a mackintosh over his uniform and, having commandeered a driver in an electricity van, asked to be let into the substation. He gained admittance, let off a thunder flash and then the 'game was up'!

Nissen huts with searchlights were positioned strategically round the village for the sighting of enemy aircraft: one at the end of Chipley Avenue, another opposite what is now White Post Nursery inside the gate, one near to Paradise Cottage and one at Bere Quarry, the base of which is still visible. These measures were thought to be necessary because of the establishment of airfields on the Blackdown Hills.

An air raid siren was positioned at the top of Church Tower – but the Rev. S. J. S. Swainson insisted that members of the Home Guard wanting to reach the top of the tower had to leave their guns at the entrance of the Church, as they should not enter a holy place bearing arms!

Evacuees

Three and half million children were evacuated from areas at risk of enemy bombing during the Second World War. Langford Budville did its bit to help. Mrs Alix Fox of Croxhall was the billeting officer for the village. At one time there were around 14 children billeted here and the Working Men's Club had to be used as an overflow classroom to accommodate such a number.

Here are some names which people have remembered:

* Brian Longworth and his mother were bombed out of Plymouth and came to live with the Percys at 4 Reynolds.
* The Wastells arrived as a family of evacuees from London and stayed in one of the old cottages up 'Blacksmith's' Lane by the Forge, where there were originally 7 or 8 cottages
* The Darbys arrived similarly with their son and daughter called Ray and Joan and stayed in 'Blacksmith's Lane'
* Ronnie & Billy Ralston – twin brothers (pictured below). One twin lived with the Percys and other with the Waygoods in Runnington.

* Rita Saunders lived with Hilda Harris
* Lilian Brown, from Leigh-on-Sea Essex, lived with Annie Broom at Church Cottage. She stayed living with her even after she had married Don Yeoman. Eventually the couple went to live in Yeovil.
* Bobby ? lived with the Westerns

* The Settles came as a family from Nottingham and lived in a cottage on a site where Coppins has been built.

In addition are these names taken from the Church's visitors book:

Royston Piggins lived with the Pikes…visited 1985

Phyllis Stimson…visited 1986

Jack Ball…visited 1988 from New Zealand

Rosemary Fletcher (now Steer)…visited 1999

Christopher Fox can remember a boy called Bill at Croxhall trying to teach him to speak cockney – much to his mother's annoyance. He also remembers Friday night being bath night for the evacuees at Croxhall.

The arrival of the evacuees must have changed the whole profile of the village. One can only assume that some were delighted to be living in the country while others would find it completely alien to their way of life. However they would all be united in their struggle to survive and cope with stringent rationing, blackouts, fear and all that the War imposed upon them. One person who was pleased was the Rev. Swainson who writes in his notes in a Record of Church Life and Affairs that between "1941-43 offertories increased owing to 'gentry' evacuees".

A Cycling Visit to no. 1 Reynolds from Alan Tucker's memoirs
– Ernest is his grandfather and Tommy his father.

In 1940 Margaret Fellows, Ernest Tucker's niece and daughter of Thomas Tucker of Parkstone, near Poole, set off for a cycling holiday of Devon with her friend Rose. She writes…

"After a comfortable night's rest and a good breakfast we set off to find Langford Budville, but first we did some shopping in Wellington as possibly we might not be having a meal at Aunty and Uncle's home. We eventually found it right in the heart of the country, real farming country. Aunty was delighted to see me after nearly 20 years, as the last time I had seen her was when she came with my Uncle to stay with us at Lilliput, Poole on their honeymoon, and I was just a school girl. Aunty was pleased to meet Rosy too and made us so welcome, and soon made tea for us and served her lovely home made cake. She said how pleased Uncle Ern will be when he comes home at 1 p.m. for his dinner. But before then Tommy arrived from the factory, his foreman had told him his cousin and her friend had stayed at their home (bed and breakfast) and so he gave Tommy permission to have the rest of the day off. Aunty insisted we stay at their home for one night or longer, Uncle too was pleased to see us and they all made us so welcome. In the afternoon Uncle showed us the big farm where he worked and Tommy showed us the pretty village. After a nice walk we returned for a lovely tea and chat. Uncle Ern was my father's youngest brother and he was so like him in his voice and ways. After tea Uncle took us to see the village church where he was sexton and also took us to the top of the church tower where we had a magnificent view of the surrounding countryside. Aunty was unable to accompany us, swollen legs caused by varicose veins prevented her from walking far, although about the house she managed wonderfully. Before returning home Uncle suggested we have a drink at their local pub. I remember Tommy going back to his home as he was underage. Uncle had a traditional

glass of cider and Rosy and I had a glass of lemonade with a dash of cider. The local folk made us most welcome. It was a quaint little inn and when Uncle told everyone where we had cycled from they were amazed. After drinking the refreshment Uncle took us back to his home a different route with a chat here and there to local farmers. So we had spent a lovely day. Also Aunty and Uncle had a lovely flower garden and such fine blooms in such rich soil and as one can imagine his vegetable garden was well stocked. We spent a lovely evening with them all and Aunty laid on a lovely supper before we retired to our bedroom where we had a comfortable nights sleep after such an interesting and exciting day. We were up in time to say farewell to Uncle and Tommy before they left for work, to thank them for making us so welcome. After having breakfast with Aunty and a little chat and thank her for such wonderful hospitality we once again set off on our cycles and, weather still excellent, we now made for Taunton and Tiverton. Everywhere we travelled we saw our wonderful troops who were back in England after the evacuation of Dunkirk. How glad they must have been to be back after all they had been through. Everywhere people were doing all they could for them."

A few of those who served

What sights they saw…what places they visited…what hardships they endured…and back home what worry and heart-ache families had to go through.

Alan Tucker writes in his memoirs about his dad:

He joined the Royal Navy on 28th October 1942 only 18 years old. His demob papers show that he was attached to HMS Raleigh – Torpoint, HMS Drake – Devonport, HMS Quebec – Loch Fyne and HMS Copra – Largs (Combined Operations Pay, Ratings and Accounts). He was an ordinary then able-bodied seaman who became a leading signaller. He was stationed at Hamworthy, Poole for a short while near to his cousin Margaret (above). During the war there was a large amphibious warfare centre there, particularly with regard to assault landing craft. Tommy was a seaman on a D Day landing craft. He was demobbed in May 1946.

He also records that his mother's three brothers served. Ernest Hayes, the eldest saw active service in the army in North Africa and Italy. Albert Hayes was a sergeant in the Military Police and Joe Hayes was in the RAF. Frank Pike, another relative, was in the Royal Navy and rose to the rank of Chief Petty Officer. Many of the female members of the family also did valuable work on the home front.

| *Tommy Tucker* | *Joe Hayes* | *Albert & Ernest in Rome* |

Sue Toomey née Pike and brother Geoff write about their dad:

Les did his Basic Training as a Royal Marine at Lympstone Barracks, near Exmouth in early 1940. He spent some time in Scotland, before sailing down to South Africa, visiting Durban amongst other places. In early 1941, he found himself on the island of Crete, where he was captured as a prisoner of war.

The prisoners were taken to the Greek mainland, before been crowded into cattle trucks, and taken on a journey lasting about 10 days, which ended near to the Polish/ Czechoslovakian border, at the Stalag V111B Camp Lamsdorf (or Teschen).

For most of his time held there, Les was used as forced labour to work underground in the nearby coal mines. Conditions were tough and grim.

As the Russian "Red" Army advanced into Poland, in early January 1945 the POWs were ordered to pack up, and were marched through Czechoslovakia, Austria and finally into Germany. The weather conditions were extremely harsh, with freezing temperatures. They walked up to 20 miles a day for nearly three months.

During this time, Les, like many others, didn't take off his boots, and at the end what was left of them, had to be cut off the men's feet.

This march has been called "The Long March to Freedom". Many didn't make it to the end of the march and liberation.

After demob in 1946, Les returned to work for the same company, Walter Gregory & Sons in Wellington, whom he had left to join the Royal Marines in 1940, and where he stayed for the rest of his working life.

He was an enthusiastic campanologist all his life, and enjoyed ringing the bells at Langford Church every Sunday for many years, as well as visiting other towers to ring out a tune!

One happy memory despite his wartime travails, which we do remember being told about as a children, was when his ship docked in Durban one Sunday morning in late 1940, he was invited to join the Cathedral bell ringing team there to ring for the Sunday service.

My father very seldom spoke of his war time experiences, and we were too young and naive to probe very much, or show any interest.

Friends who had known him before the War, described him then as a vibrant man and active sportsman, but said he returned afterwards as " a shadow of his former self ".

In happier times –

Roger Wotton writes about his dad:

*'My father Jack was in the RAF and part of the British Expeditionary Force. Unfortu-
nately he was cut off from Dunkirk and was posted missing for 9 months until escaping
through western France and eventually back to England. But, as is so often the case, he
never talked about it and it is only in the last 2 years that I have found out, long after the
chance to talk to him about it has gone.'*

Victor Wood and George Bennett saw active service during the war and, it would appear,
were the only ones killed who came from the village. Their names are commemorated
on a plaque in the village church and are read out each year at the Remembrance Day
service. Alan Tucker traced their cause of death:

Victor Frederick Wood was a Private in the The Buffs (Royal East Kent Regiment) 4th
Bn and died aged 25 between 23/10/1943 and 24/10/1943 – his name is remembered
on the Athens Memorial. He was the son of Ernest Fredrick and Ivy Wood, husband of
Marjorie Glynne Wood, of Taunton, Somerset.

George Bennett was in the Merchant Navy serving as a donkeyman (stoker) on
the S.S. Sirikishna (Leith). He died aged 31 on 24/2/1941. He is remembered on the
Tower Hill Memorial. He was the son of Ernest Bennett and Annie Bennett. It is
reported that at 02.20 hours on 24th February, 1941, the Sirikishna (Master Robert
Paterson), dispersed from convoy OB-288, was hit on the port side amidships by one
torpedo from U-96 south of Iceland and was abandoned by the crew. The U-boat first
had to load a torpedo from an upper deck container into the boat because all other
torpedoes were spent. At 08.36 hours, a *coup de grâce* was fired that hit amidships and
caused the ship to sink rapidly after breaking in two. She was the ship of the convoy
commodore Rear Admiral R.A.A. Plowden DSO. The master, the commodore, five
naval staff members, 34 crew members and two gunners were lost.

With young men disappearing into the armed forces there was an acute shortage of
labour in the country and for many girls call-up meant a choice of either joining the Armed
Forces or the Land Army. Production lines at Foxes turned over to khaki and air force blue
for service uniforms so once again the female labour force was in great demand.

1941 saw the first American troops arrive in the south west. David Mainhood of
Oddmeads recollects that the Oddmeads field was filled with American tanks for a
few days and made an awful mess. He also remembers that the vicar and his wife from
Nynehead were bombed out and billeted at the house for a short while. The bomb had
mistakenly been dropped by an allied plane very near to the Vicarage doing significant
damage to the roof and the windows. The pilot had been instructed to try and jettison a
jammed bomb on Langford Heathfield. Later on towards D-day people recall infantry
manoeuvres taking place on Langford Heathfield.

Churchill's Victory Speech 8th May 1945:

Was everyone glued to their radio in Langford Budville? One can only begin to feel what it must have felt like to hear these words.

'God bless you all. This is your victory. It is the victory of the cause of freedom in every land. In all our long history we have never seen a greater day than this. Everyone, man or woman, has done their bit. Everyone has tried. Neither the long years nor the dangers, nor the fierce attacks of the enemy, have in any way weakened the independent resolve of the British Nation. God Bless you all!'

Victory celebations in Langford Budville

Wellington Weekly News 23rd May 1945

VE celebrations were continued on Whit Monday but perforce many of the outdoor events, including sports on the Common, had to be cancelled. A bountiful tea for the children was laid in the Workmen's Club after which a series of indoor games and sports were fully enjoyed. During the evening Mr Stan Rowland, fittingly attired with top hat and cigar, impersonated the Prime Minister and after speaking to the children presented the prizes… music was supplied by Mr. W.F. Harris (violin), Miss E. Crowcombe (piano). Articles of food were auctioned by Major M. Sanford. Community dancing and singing followed and a happy time ended with 'Auld Lang Syne' and the National Anthem'.

Chapter 4 – FAMILY CONNECTIONS

The Sanford Connection
John Lloyd

27th February 2012
Dear Marjorie Stockley
In answer to your request about my life in Langford Budville –

I married my first wife Joy (Sanford) in 1951. She was actually born in London in 1931 the daughter of Captain Ayshford Sanford and Rosemary Sanford (née Lindsay) but her birth certificate address is Langford Court. The house was sold in 1949; by an extraordinary stroke of timing I sold my business in London in 1964 and bought back Langford Court. You can imagine Joy's excitement returning to the house where she had spent her first years. She sadly died in 1967 leaving four children Serena, Richard, Lucy and Jonathan.

I married again in 1970 to Penelope Astley-Rushton of Cothay Manor. Penny was a wonderful support to me in all the positions I held in Langford Budville and Somerset and a brilliant hostess at Langford Court for so many things - St. Peter's Church, St. John's Ambulance, Somerset Branch of the Coldstream Guards Association, also, as she was a Catholic, her own church in Wellington. This was in addition to frequently opening the garden under the National Garden Scheme as well as the renowned Remembrance Day Parties after the service at St. Peter's Church. Penny died in 2002.

Richard my older son, his wife Jane and their four daughters moved into Langford Court in 2004 – much to the delight of all the family.

You asked about my war service during the Second World War. It was with the Coldstream Guards from 1942-1947. I was awarded the Military Cross in the winter of 1944 during the Italian campaign fighting in the Appenine Mountains 10 miles south of Bologna. My platoon was in an isolated position, at the foot of Monte Sole, when we were attacked by troops of the 16 S.S. Division, just before dawn on the 27th December 1944. My platoon all deserved to win the award.

Positions I held in Somerset:
Justice of the Peace (Taunton Branch) – 21 years
St. John's Ambulance – held various positions over a period of 40 years, finishing up as Chairman of the Council
President of the Coldstream Guards Association (Yeovil and Taunton Branch Somerset) – 40 years
Somerset Association of Boys Clubs – 7 years
High Sheriff of Somerset 1976
Deputy Lieutenant 1986
In Langford Budville I was Church Warden for 25 years and Chairman of the Parish Council for 21 years. I remember with particular pleasure that the Council played a pivotal role in purchasing the Triangle from the Nynehead Court Estate for use as a recreation area for the children, that the school was saved from closure in 1988 and that we won the Best Kept Village in Somerset competition in 1989. A plaque commemorates the latter

on the wall of The Old Post Office above the Domesday plaque which acknowledges our inclusion in the Domesday Book of 1086.

I hope I have managed to answer your questions sufficiently and wish you well with the publication of the History Book.

Yours sincerely
John Lloyd

William, William Ayshford & Joy Sanford at Chipley Park c1938

John Lloyd c 1950

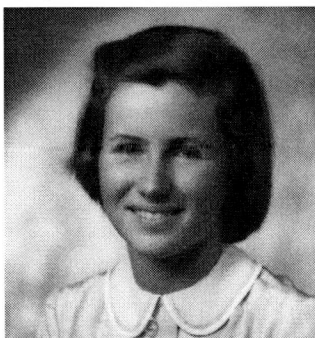

Joy Sanford c1946

Serena, Lucy & Richard at Langford Court c1967

Official Visit to St. Peter's Church as High Sheriff of Somerset by Captain John Lloyd & Mrs Penelope Lloyd 1976 – photographed with the vicar, the Reverend Howard Bowen

The Fox Connection

Christopher Fox remembers his parents:

Alexandra (Alix) Fox *1909-97*

My mother was born in Rangoon, Burma and later lived in Buckinghamshire. She came to Wellington as an art student in the late 1920's to help with the decoration of the interior of the newly built chapel at Wellington School. She married Thomas Fox of Oldway House, Wellington in 1930 and they set up home at Croxhall in Langford Budville, where she lived for almost 67 years until her death. She joined the W.I. in the 1930's as a young wife and mother, and remained a member all her life. She was an expert at needlework, craftwork and embroidery and used to demonstrate these to W.I. groups throughout the county.

The outbreak of World War Two brought more responsibilities with the need to produce and preserve all kinds of foodstuffs grown in members' gardens and allotments. She was appointed Billeting Officer for the area, and was responsible for finding homes for children evacuated from the bombing in London and other cities. Her home was a warm and welcoming place, not only for the evacuees but also for a constant stream of family and friends and their children. She was a founder member of the Langford Ladies in 1965, as well as a handicraft group in the village which still works for the benefit of its members, the Church and the community. She was also a fine artist in both oils and water-colours, and a founder member of the Wellington Art Group. Over the years, her pictures – mostly landscapes of the Somerset countryside – have been exhibited at art shows in all parts of the county. She was a keen and skilful gardener, with a wide knowledge of plants and flowers, and she loved all kinds of literature, especially poetry. Her Christian faith, which she nurtured in all her four children, found expression in a lifetime of service to Christian causes, especially the YWCA and the Bible Society. In her memory her family have donated copies of the Revised English Bible to the church, so that the congregation can follow the readings during the service.

Thomas Fox *1902-88*

A member of the Fox family, who were responsible for bringing prosperity to Wellington through the woollen trade in the 19th century, my father was the fifth oldest son of an oldest son to be named Thomas. Educated at Monkton Combe School he went to Cambridge to read Chemistry. Being unable to finish the course due to the untimely death of his father he joined the family business in Tonedale with particular responsibility for dyeing and finishing. He married my mother in Tylers Green in Buckinghamshire in May 1930 and their two boys were born in 1931 and 1934 and the 2 girls in 1937 and 1944. When the 2nd World War broke out, the production of uniform cloths was stepped up and shift working was introduced. After doing a morning shift at Tonedale, Tom would walk to the headquarters of the Home Guard in what is still the headquarters of the Somerset Cadet Battalion (The Rifles) ACF, where he then worked as Platoon Commander and Adjutant of F (Wellington) Coy. In his spare time, he designed and made safe fuses for petrol bombs to be used against tanks and transport in the event of an invasion, and he also helped the civilian authorities in updating and testing the gas masks that everyone had to carry.

Like his wife he involved himself in the Church and its many activities. He taught himself to work in brass and silver and found many things in the Church which needed to be replaced or repaired; perhaps, sad to say, to the neglect of DIY that was needed in the house! He restored the altar and sanctuary candlesticks, the brass memorial plaques on the walls – providing oak frames where necessary.

In the late forties, the Church was wired for electricity and Bill Percy, with my father's moral support, installed the present lights. Later, when the vicar was winding the mechanical clock, a wire broke sending two tons of cast iron crashing to the floor of the tower, leading to the present electrical control system being installed with Tom Fox's help. When the previous wooden flagpole broke he made and erected the present steel one.

In the sixties he acquired a lot of candle ends and later nearly two hundredweight of paraffin wax. He made a number of moulds of different sizes and all the equipment needed and taught himself to make candles, which he returned to the Churches who had given him the ends. He extended this service to Wells and Exeter Cathedrals, developing a unique system for casting beeswax.

For over twenty years he was a Church Warden and also Treasurer of the Working Men's Club.

Thomas and Alix Fox c1975

Christopher Fox also worked for Foxes and for many years was a Church Warden – and still makes candles!

The Cottrell Connection

A Farming Family from an article entitled Somerset Farming Personalities 1960

After starting on a hill country farm near Culmstock and then moving to Fordbridge (part of the Ashburton Estate), Milverton in 1914, Tom Cottrell purchased South Gundenham in 1927 and also rented North Gundenham from that time from the Nynehead Estate. In the early thirties he started selling milk to households in Wellington ladling milk from a churn which was carried in the back of a pony and trap.

His son Jim Cottrell spent the beginning of his working career in Agricultural Engineering but returned to farm in 1932, mainly due to a remark by his father that they were short-handed. In 1935 Jim married and started off with 60 acres farming part of North Gundenham Farm.

In 1949 the Nynehead Estate was sold to Bolnore Estates, who in turn gave the tenants the opportunity to buy their farms. Tom took the opportunity of purchasing North Gundenham and after a brief interval sold it to Jim. In 1959 Jim's two sons David & Roger joined in the business as directors of a limited company under the name James Cottrell & Sons (Langford) Limited. Shortly afterwards he was able to buy Bere Farm situated within a mile of North Gundenham. His son David was married in March 1960 and took over responsibility of Bere farm. Still at home are younger daughter Mary and son John aged 16 who is settling down to work on the farm.

*   *   *

Sadly 50 years later Roger and Mary are no longer with us and David has retired from farming, although he still lives at Bere Farm. John (the youngest of Jim's three sons and on the far right in the family picture) and his wife Heather currently live at North Gundenham and the Gundenham Dairies website states that they have 'a herd of 350 Holstein Friesians and farm 500 acres of prime Somerset pasture land'. Tom would certainly be very proud of his children and grandchildren's achievements and that John's son, Ian, the fourth generation of Cottrell farmers in Langford Budville, is following in their footsteps.

Tom and Ellen Cottrell at South Gundenham

Jim and Winifred's wedding 1935

Cottrell family – David, Jim, Winifred, Mary, Roger, Jock the dog, John in 1960

The Brewers & Jones Connection

The Brewers

Gerald Brewer and Valerie Pitman (née Brewer) were both born at home in Langford Budville and still live in the village today. As far as we are aware no one else can currently lay claim to this status. Of course years ago, because of the lack of opportunity, transport etc. there would have been many more who would have been born and lived all their lives in the same village.

This side of the Brewer family came to the village when William Brewer, born in Milverton, married Martha Taylor, born in Langford Budville and the third generation of Taylors in the village, in 1870 in the parish church of St. Peter's. The photo overleaf shows William and Martha with their 10 children.

On the census of 1881 he appears as a head gardener living at Bowerings Cottages (now known as Rose Cottages), by 1891 he has moved to a large house near the church and is a pork butcher and carrier. In 1901 he is described as a farmer; the location of his farm is unclear although it may have been part of Peter's Mead. In Kelly's directory he is logged from 1897-1919 as a Horse and Trap Proprietor. Kelly also notes that he is caretaker for the Working Men's Reading Room in 1883. This is an indication of how multi-skilled and flexible people had to be to earn a living and sustain a large family.

Brewer family c1898/99
Back row *Tom, John (Jack), Alice, William Henry, Mary, Beatrice.* Front row *Edith, Martha, Mabel, Minnie, William, Annie (Nancy)*

William Brewer and daughter Beatrice in a trap near to Langford Court c1920

Elizabeth Cornish, William H. Brewer, Wilson Brewer, youngest son with dog Chum in the garden of their cottage c 1935 later to be pulled down to make way for 1 & 2 Chapelview

Beatrice never married but became a woman of property and by 1916 owned the row of five Rose Cottages. When her parents died she went to live in London with her sister Alice and died intestate in 1938 then just owning two of the properties.

William Henry Brewer, eldest son, was born in 1871 in Langford Budville and lived his entire life in the village. He married Elizabeth Cornish in 1895 and had seven children: Gilbert, Harold – Gerald's father, Gladys, Wilfred, Cyril – Valerie's father, Lionel and Wilson.

A fitting tribute for just one of the many antecedents:

I feel privileged to be asked to write a few lines about Wilson Brewer. I have not known anyone who was more a centre part of a village community than Wilson was in Langford Budville. Here was a strong extrovert, and above all a joyful 'character' who gave so much to our village in warmth and laughter, and friendliness, and song.

He loved to sing wherever he was – he sang at work, and anyone who has been privileged to attend Chapel will know how he sang there; many too will remember his singing at the Old Age Pensioners Christmas Dinners. He would stop and talk to anyone wherever he happened to be, always friendly and warm and kind...

So writes John Lloyd in the Parish Magazine 18th November 1981

Would that perhaps we could all be remembered in this way.

The Australian Connection
– sharing a great, great grandfather

Heather Schefe emails from Gympie, Queensland, Australia:

I am the custodian of a 'black coat' which family myth says belonged to my great grandfather's uncle, William Brewer (seated in the old photograph above) and affectionately known by family as Uncle Griz. The story goes that at the age of seventeen his nephew (William G. Brewer Stephens) emigrated to Australia to join his other 'Brewer' uncles in search of a better life. He returned briefly to England in 1898 where he found the climate so cold that he was given the 'black coat' by Uncle Griz and returned with it to Gympie, Queensland. The conjecture is that it could well have been made at Foxes or one of the district's woollen mills over 115 years ago.

In my quest to find my ancestors I had made contact with Lorna Gibbs (née Jones – her great-grandmother was Minnie Brewer) on the internet. On a trip to the UK in 2009 we met at St. Peter's Church and as a parting gesture I signed the visitor's book noting my connection with the Brewer family. Six months later I received a phone call from Valerie Pitman (née Brewer) who had found this entry. With her help and that of her cousin Janet Read

Heather Schefe in the 'black coat'

(née Brewer) the nameless in photographs became people. The rest as they say is history as the search led to another trip to Langford Budville when my husband and I stayed with Valerie and John Pitman. We hope to welcome them to Australia very soon to see the 'black coat'.

The Jones

Ernest Jones was apprenticed as wheelwright to Alfred Leatt of Langford Budville in 1905 and in 1913 married Minnie Brewer.

Indenture certificate

His son Aubrey born in 1914 also became a wheelwright, carpenter and undertaker and between them they made 72 coffins. People remember them delivering coffins in the side-car of their motorbike which must have been an interesting sight.

Aubrey (left) & Ernest (right) working behind No.1 Rose Cottage c 1935

Aubrey married Bet Whaites (a cook at Langford Court) in 1920 and had sons Brian and Glyn. Initially they lived in No 2 Rose Cottages before moving to Wiseborough but returning in 1959 to Yew Tree which Aubrey had had built. Glyn has been the keeper of many family artefacts and tools connected with the carpentry trade and displayed them at the 2011 Village Fete.

Glyn Jones in the History Tent at the Langford Village Fete 2011

Gilbert Jones (brother to Ernest) married Annie (née Brewer) in 1909. Their son Raymond married Phyllis Ware – seen in the Village School chapter Class of 1953 with their son Michael on her knee. I was privileged to meet 'Auntie Phil' just before she died aged 101. This is Lorna's (who met Heather on the internet) great grandmother.

Hope you are managing to follow all this intertwining. Perhaps this is sufficient to whet the appetite for anyone who wishes to pursue the connections.

The Tucker Connection

From Alan Tucker's memoirs:

Ernest Tucker, my grandfather, was born on September 11 1885 at Clayhanger, Devon. Ernest's life was to be marred by family tragedies. By 1901 he had left home and moved to Hayne Moor at nearby Bampton where he boarded with William Chidgey, a rabbit trapper. By 1904 he was living at Huntsham and working in the gardens at Huntsham Court. On January 21 1907 Ernest married Annie Yarde at St Nicholas Church, Kittisford. It is not clear when Ernest decided to leave Huntsham to cross the border into Somerset and become established at Kittisford, then Langford Budville. Langford in 1911 was a small village with a population of only 351. Four children followed the marriage, all born at Langford Budville. Sadly all four, Frederick, John or 'Jack', Gertude Annie, and Millicent, had died as young children by 1918.

In 1916 two important events took place. Ernest had not joined up when the war broke out as he was holding down a farm job, an occupation that made its own contribution to the war effort. He was also 31 years of age and had a young family. In 1916 conscription was progressively introduced to different categories of men. Ernest was granted exemption from military service on domestic grounds as his wife was 'in consumption' and 'if called up his children would have no-one to care for them'. On January 3 1917 a report on Ernest's domestic circumstances showed that he was now working at Fox's factory at Wellington and Annie was subject to 'convulsive attacks'. She was also very deaf and had four young children aged 6, 4, 3 and 1.

Annie's medical condition can be deduced from the other family event of 1916. On Saturday October 21 the family cottage burnt down. The Wellington Weekly News reported details of the circumstances of the fire. The cottage was one of an adjoining pair close to the Gospel Hall and nearly opposite the Working Men's Club. In one cottage lived Henry Hayes and his wife and grandchild and in the other 'Mr and Mrs Tucker'. Henry Hayes worked on the Nynehead estate and coincidentally was later to become my maternal great grandfather. The cottages, which were both gutted, were thatched with brick tiles at the back of the building and belonged to the Nynehead Estate. A possible chimney spark started a fire on that morning but by the time the firemen and their horse-drawn engine had arrived from Wellington, 'as no adequate water supply was available the Brigade could do little except to assist in removing furniture etc from the burning houses'. Most of the contents of the Tuckers' house were saved and moved to the Working Men's Club. A consumptive shelter erected at the rear of the building was undamaged. (The shelter still stands at the rear of the Old Chapel garden). The two homeless families moved temporarily to an empty Sanford residence called 'Odd Meads' a few hundred yards away and the Tuckers later moved to a cottage behind the blacksmiths near the site of what later became 'Ware's bungalow'.

At Christmas 1918 local members of the Agricultural Labourers' Union raised a subscription to help the grieving parents of the children who had died. A year later further disaster struck when on November 29 1919 Annie Tucker, died, aged 31. The Wellington Weekly News stated that in a "period of less than five years he (Ernest) had lost all four of his children, his mother, a sister and now his wife. In addition he has been burnt out of house and home. There can be few men in the district who have had such a chapter of misfortunes". At the time of his wife's death Ernest Tucker was living at Gundenham, a small hamlet on the road between Langford Budville and Wellington.

In 1923 he was married for the second time to Lucy Ann Pike. Lucy had been born at Langford Budville, Somerset, on November 2 1886, the daughter of Samuel Pike, an agricultural labourer, and Anne Pike. At the time of the 1881 census the Pike family was living at Stones Cottage (now known as Paradise Cottage).

On April 6 1924 the marriage produced their only child, Samuel Thomas 'Tommy' Tucker, my father. Ernest was still a farm labourer, living at Gundenham. In 1926 he was able to move his new family into the first of the new 'Wheatley Act' council houses at Langford Budville - No 1, Reynolds. During the Depression Ernest supplemented his wages by acting as sexton to the parish church at Langford Budville. At some point, probably in the 1920s, Ernest began work at Middle Chipley Farm, where he worked until his retirement.

After retiring from farm work Ernest Tucker became a gardener at Langford Court, where I can remember him at work in the mid-1950s. Ernest's son, 'Tommy', and his wife, Eunice Hayes, my mother, also lived at 1, Reynolds, Langford Budville, after their marriage in 1948. On May 26 1955 Lucy Ann Tucker, my paternal grandmother, died and a year later Ernest moved to Milverton with his son's family, where he died on 1st January 1961. Ernest rarely missed Bampton Fair, the annual pony fair, and took me along on one occasion by train from Milverton.

'Tommy' attended the local village school and by 1940 was working at Fox's woollen factory. He joined the Royal Navy on October 28, 1942, still only 18 years old. His demob papers show that he was attached to Raleigh, Drake, Quebec and Copra; the latter from August 1943 until demob in May 1946. After his return to Langford Budville Tommy married my mother, Eunice Charlotte Hayes who was born on September 1 1923 at Langford Budville. The wedding was on July 17 1948 in the local church. Within a year I was born on July 14 1949 and, three years later, my brother, Michael, on June 16 1952. In 1956 the family moved from 1 Reynolds, Langford Budville, to 'Old Halls', a large house at nearby Milverton. I continued my contact with Langford Budville by attending the local school until I was eleven.

Lucy Ann Pike and her four brothers with her parents, Sam and Annie Pike, my great-grandparents.

Ern Tucker, grandfather, with his first wife Annie Tucker née Yarde and three of their children.

Ern Tucker, grandfather, with me at Bampton Fair in the 1950s.

The Salway Connection

Carol Tucker remembers her grandfather Fred Salway 1876 -1947

Fred Salway was born in 1876 in Dunkeswell – son of Samuel (later carpenter at Chipley Park) and Alice Salway. He was admitted to Langford Budville School in June 1879 (Binns' Register). In the 1891 census he is recorded as an Apprentice Printer living with his parents at Shattocks. (Thomas (agricultural labourer) and Jane Stone (launderess) were their next door neighbours.)

When Fred was 21 he had received a severe kick on his ankle playing football, neglected it and it turned tubercular. He worked in the printing department of the Wellington Weekly News, walking to and from Langford Budville every day in spite of his injured ankle An office collection enabled him to receive treatment at Bart's, where the son of Dr. Randolph of Milverton was a student and interested in his case. Pioneering surgery meant that he had only his ankle bone removed instead of his whole foot.

Fred married Jane (Jin) Watson, one of the 'dust-hunters' in Bindon House in 1908. The other pair at the double wedding ceremony were Lily Watson (Jin's sister), another house maid from Bindon, and Walter Perry, employed at Fox Brothers' Mills in Tonedale, Wellington.

My grandparents lived for a short while in Bovet Street, Wellington until their house was built in the village. They lived the rest of their married life in Rose Cottage, one of the row of semi-detached Edwardian houses, just up from the Martlet Inn. Brother Frank lived a few doors away at Copplestones where he and his wife Emily ran a general store. Walter Perry came to live next door to Fred at Myrtle Cottage.

Fred had two children Alison Marguerite (my mum) 24th December 1911 and Philip Watson on 18th December 1914.

Between the wars Fred and a reporter from the Wellington Weekly News joined the Union and were instantly dismissed. He later worked on the printing staff for Radiac Shirt Works, Taunton for Messrs. McIntyre, Hogg, Marsh and Co. He still walked daily to Wellington, catching the bus from there to Taunton.

He was well known and respected in the area. He was clerk to the Langford Budville Parish Council from 1931 until his death in 1947 and was also a sidesman at St. Peter's Church.

Fred Salway taken at Weston-super-Mare 1936

The Braddick Connection

Robert Hayes remembers his grandfather William Stephen Braddick 1879-1963

William Stephen (Bill) Braddick was born 12th January 1879 at Chadshunt, Warwickshire, the first of six children born to William and Fanny Braddick, who lived at Thorne St. Margaret. A keen sportsman in his younger days he played rugby and cricket for Langford Budville, Nynehead and Wellington, where he captained the Wellington Home Team for a number of years. He sang in the choir at All Saints Church, Rockwell Green, and St. Peter's Church, Langford Budville for the greater part of his life. He was churchwarden of the latter for some years.

At the age of 22 the 1901 census describes him as a presser in a woollen factory employed by Elworthy Bros at Westford, Rockwell Green. He was married twice; firstly at Nynehead Church, to Florence Gollap in 1903. They lived in Wellington until their first child Iris was born in 1907 and it was about this time he had Heathfield Cottage, Langford Budville built. They lived there until their marriage ended in 1916. (Iris became a teacher at the Village Primary School and married Wilfred Brewer.)

In 1917 he married Elsie Edith Emma Mitchell and they settled at Heathfield Cottage, where they had four children; Hubert, Mary (my mum), Elizabeth and Geoffrey.

In 1934 the factory at Westford closed and Bill found himself unemployed at the age of 55. William C.A. Sanford (Lord of the Manor) offered a field and one cow rent free for one year to 'see how he got on'. This proved to be a worthwhile venture as at the time of his death in 1963, having purchased land in 1949 from the Bolnore Estate sale, Ritherdons Farm had grown to 95 acres with 20 milking cows.

Bill Braddick c1950

Florence Braddick with daughter Iris c1909 outside Heathfield Cottage

Chapter 5 – **BOYHOOD MEMORIES**

Robert Hayes' school holidays – Down on the Farm

My father was the third child of James and Mary Hayes of Higher Ritherdons Cottage, Langford Budville, and my mother was the third child of William and Elsie Braddick, of Heathfield Cottage. They spent their early married years living in Higher Ritherdons Cottage with my grandmother Mary Ann Hayes. By the time I was born they had moved to a house at Milverton, but Mum continued to help out on my grandfather's farm and would put me on the back of her bicycle and ride to Langford Budville.

Higher Ritherdons Cottage stood opposite my grandfather Braddick's farmyard, which was up the road from Langford Court, and an old thatched cob cottage once occupied by Tommy Taylor. Dad described Tommy as leaning against his front door smoking a pipe, and being able to "spit a ring around a sixpence". As a boy, Dad and his brother Albert would toss stones down Tommy's chimney hoping they would give out a loud crack when they split in the fire giving Tommy a fright as he snoozed in his chair. The cottage is no longer there and, sadly, neither is Higher Ritherdons which burned down in the 1950s.

Tommy Taylor's old cottage was a two up two down and after it was vacated my grandfather used to store his harvested potato crop there. The potatoes were stored in the bigger of the two downstairs rooms. The fire place had an old iron range in which mum would light a fire to keep us warm, while she sorted over stored potatoes and bagged them up ready to be sold. Most of my time was spent running around the farm, climbing on bales of hay and chasing wild cats about the place. I remember one of my earliest culinary delights was a baked potato that Mum would drop into the fire, to be retrieved and rolled around like a cat with a ball of wool until it was cool enough to peel off the outer charred skin ready to eat.

It wasn't long before my older brother William and I started at primary school and, as Mum had started working at Fox Bros in Wellington in the mending rooms, the problem of what to do with us during the school holidays was solved by catching the Western National bus to spend the day with our grandparents on the farm. We would get off at Langford Budville and Mum carried on to Wellington, collecting us when the bus returned in the afternoon.

The day usually started by feeding the chickens and calves in the yard next to Heathfield (where 4 bungalows now stand above the Martlet Inn), milk for the calves and yesterday's table scraps and corn for the chickens. The next job was to collect the eggs from the laying boxes in the chicken houses. We would put a handful of straw in the bottom of a bucket and pick the eggs up moving from house to house and if we knew anywhere that the chickens were laying in the barns collect them as well.

After we had had our breakfast (hopefully a double-yolked egg) we would go with Jack Wood to fetch Blacky the cart horse and Jack would hitch him up to a wagon ready to collect kale or mangels. The mangels were often stacked by my grandfather in a clamp on the wide grass verge opposite the Jubilee seat and covered with a thick layer of bracken taken from the common. The wagon would be loaded up with mangels and taken to the field to feed the cows. I would sit up the front of the wagon and Jack Wood would tell Blacky to "walk on" while he would stand in the back throwing the mangels or kale off the back. We would then return to the farm yard where the wagon was un-hitched and stored and take Blacky to his field (usually below Paradise Cottage over the common) with me riding bareback hanging on to his mane for dear life.

With the cows fed, the rest of the day was usually spent getting up to mischief. We would spend hours on the common or down by the river at Wellisford, looking for birds' nests, building camps, making bows and arrows etc. I can remember being terrified of the adders on the common. If we were really lucky we would find a discarded skin but if we were unlucky we would come across an adder basking in the warm sunshine! Someone would shout "Adder" and we would all scatter in different directions.

But for me one of the highlights was to spend time in the blacksmith's watching Charlie Wood, who was a short stout man as wide as he was tall. He always wore a cloth cap, leather apron, collarless shirt and braces, with his sleeves rolled up. To enter his forge was to walk into a room lined with every shade of black imaginable. The only light apart from the doorway was a small window to one side of the door. The fire was in the middle of the room with a large set of bellows to one side. I would spend a lot of the time pumping a foot operated grindstone holding an old nail against it to set off an amazing trail of sparks across the corner of the shop. It never seemed to bother Charlie one bit.

Charlie seemed to be the one man in the village who was called upon to repair almost anything but his main function was shoeing horses. They would arrive at the forge and be tied up just outside the door in a covered area. Charlie would set about his task with his customary phrase of "bide still 'orse". Having removed the old shoes he would heat and fashion the new shoe and place it on the horse's foot only to disappear in a cloud of smoke. Charlie could be heard, if not always seen, puffing and snorting as he adjusted the shoe for the best fit.

One of the amazing things about life in Langford Budville during this time was the endless trail of tradesmen that called at the house. All of the following would arrive at some time during the week in their vans – butcher, baker, grocer, fishmonger, paraffin man, coal man – not forgetting the library van.

In the afternoon we would collect the cows and take them over to Ritherdon's farmyard for milking. As a child it always amazed me how all these cows remembered where to go in the milking stalls in the barn. If Uncle Geoffrey Braddick wasn't available then Norman Wood, or Jack Wood (not related) would be in charge. Jack was the son of Charlie Wood the blacksmith. Norman Wood will forever be remembered by me for being a good shot with his improvised milk pistol straight from the cow's udder. If I got too close he would turn the cow's teat and catch me every time.

As soon as the milk had been taken from the cow it was carried to the milking parlour and poured into the header tank above the cooler – a sort of water cooled radiator. The milk would trickle over the surface of the radiator and through a muslin lined funnel and into the milk churns ready to be put on the churn-stand to be collected by the milk lorry, not forgetting some milk set to one side in a churn lid to feed the many cats. The cows were then returned to the field.

And we would return wearily back to Milverton on the bus. Those were the days!

At other times:

A lot of the local villagers (Mums and children eager to earn pin or pocket money) would turn up to help Grandfather harvest his potato crop. Uncle Geoff would drive the tractor along the rows of potatoes with the "spinner" on the back. This would throw the potatoes on the surface *of the ground and the assembled workforce would bag up the potatoes ready for collection. They would then be taken back to the farm and stored in the old cottage next to the farm.*

There were always mushrooms to be picked in Crownfield. Grandmother would take them to Wellington to be sold and this would provide welcome pocket money for my brother and me.

We would also help to pick the cider apples in the Middle Orchard (below the school and part of Swifts). The apples were washed in a large galvanized tank and taken back to the cider house located opposite Heathfield Cottage, where today there are two large wooden doors. This was the entrance to where Grandfather kept his cider press and all the barrels to store the cider.

Harvest Time in the 50s
Roger Wotton

The threshing machine used to do the rounds of the farms in the summer, and as boys we could follow its route into the village by the marks left on the road by the steel rimmed wheels. It was positioned in Crown Field, opposite The Martlet, the corn threshed and the straw put into ricks. I seem to remember most people turned out to help. I am sure that the pub used to slake a few thirsts after a days threshing, which was very dusty work. The corn was brought to the machine, initially by horse and cart; Blackie and Smart were two horses that I remember, owned by Mr Braddick. I also remember being thrown off Smart when taking her back to the field at night, when she took it into her mind to have a bit of a gallop. As I grew older, I used to tread the load (placing the straw around the cart), and then as I grew stronger, I would be the one pitching the straw or hay onto the cart – all part of being a country boy. The Harvest Festival Service was always on a Friday night and the windows were decorated with produce, sheaves of corn etc. The church was packed full, even farmers who didn't step inside the church from one Festival to another would attend to bring the harvest home. On one hot occasion, with the door thrown open, the singing was reported to have been heard on the Runnington road.

Chapter 6 – **NOTABLE BUILDINGS**

Langford Court *c1487*

Langford Court was probably for most of its life a substantial farmhouse. It was occupied by the Ritherdon family, who were significant landowners in Langford Budville, from at least as far back as the 1640s and for well over 100 years afterwards. The property became known as Ritherdons, and was so called until the 1870s when it became Langford Court for about 20 years before reverting again to Ritherdons and then back again to Langford Court in the 1920s. Ownership of the property passed into the hands of the Ayshford Sanford family when they acquired the rights to the Manor of Langford Budville in 1829.

In origin a mediaeval building, it has been much modified over the centuries. It is likely that, in the original house, much or all of the ground floor was open to the roof in the manner of a great hall, with open-hearth heating. The upper floor seems to have been added in stages, with a westward extension in the 17th century. In the early 18th century, a rear wing was added and the exterior of the premises was probably renovated at the same time. The house was extended westward again on at least one occasion in the 18th or 19th centuries to reach its present dimensions. A stained glass window in the staircase bears the Ayshford crest and was made by John Toms of Wellington in 1851, who also produced stained glass for the St Peter's Church.

The 1841 census records the farming Hitchcock family in residence – husband, wife, 7 children, 2 servants and an older lady (possibly the farmer's mother-in-law). By 1861 the Curate of Langford Budville, Rev. W H Walrond was living there and, in the 1870s, Major John de Haviland occupied the property. Major de Haviland's family had earlier lived at Gundenham. The Ayshford Sanfords moved in as owner/occupiers for a short period in the 1930s while waiting for Chipley Park to be vacated. They were followed by John Van Heusen (possible connection to the Taunton shirt-making factory). The Van Heusen's were hosts to the 1935 Silver Jubilee celebration party at Langford Court. A number of other tenants followed before Langford Court was sold by Bolnore Estates in 1949 as part of the dispersal of the Sanford estate. However, it is now once again owned and occupied by a descendant of the Sanford family – see Family Connections.

The house today – back view

The house today – north east corner

Stained glass window

Hill View

Built possibly c1600 close to the churchyard as a house from which the churchwardens could distribute the 'holy loaf' after Sunday services. As their 'own sign of the times' they decorated some of the walls with plaster mouldings. The carved head of a mitred bishop and a bearded man can still be seen. In conjunction with the 'Poor House' which burnt down in 1908 it is thought to have been used as a kind of church hall, briefly as a school and until 1834 to house the old and poor of the parish. It was probably sold to raise money for the parish quota towards the cost of building the Wellington Workhouse and on the 1843 tithe map it was described as a 'house and shop owned by James Holway'

The photo shows the iron railings which would probably have been commandeered in the second World War.

c1930s – Mary Ann Stone – Hill View

Mary Ann's daughter Annie (Broom) inherited the property and lived there for 80 years until 1984.

The Old Forge *c1602*

The Old Forge – today

Bindon House *c1650*

The discovery of Neolithic weapons and tools at Bindon suggest that a settlement might have existed at the site 4,000 years ago.

The name, which means 'the hill where beans grow', is thought to be Saxon in origin. However, there are no known traces of those early years and, although the Domesday Book records the manors of Langford, Wellisford and Milverton, there is no mention of Bindon. The earliest documentary evidence is a reference in 1237 to Hugh de Wendene – also spelt Bendene or Bendone, and believed to be a form of Bindon. Another document of the time states that William de Longespée, grandson of Henry II, confirmed Hugh de Bendene's right to land in Langford. William, a crusader, was killed in the great Christian defeat of Mansourah in 1250. Various other documents refer to the de Bendone family up to the 14th century, although it seems likely that the estate passed at some time to the Chipplegh family (of Chipley).

By 1520 the owner of the estate was named Humphrey Calwoodleigh. The Calwoodleighs were an important family in the South West of England, Humphrey's father having been an MP and Mayor of Exeter on at least 3 occasions.

The Calwoodleighs were followed by the Malets, another prestigious local family, who were to hold it for nearly 200 years. Some documents belonging to the Order of the Augustinians of the Assumption, which owned the property during the Second World War, are said to provide evidence that Bindon was 'a centre of clandestine Royalist activity' during the 17th century although this seems improbable given the Malets were strongly opposed to Papist influences.

Another tale from this era helps to date the present house more accurately. In the early 1680's, John Trenchard MP, an ardent follower of the pretender to the Crown, the Duke of Monmouth, visited a 'recently built' house with a stone staircase four miles north of Wellington. From a window he allegedly observed the Devon Militia exercising in church fields. This almost certainly refers to Bindon as the core of the house is mid

1600's, its stone staircase surviving till c1880, and there is a window from which there is a sightline to Wellington Church, although today obscured by trees.

The Malets' long association with Bindon ended in 1701 when it was sold – possibly to fund the deposit for a business venture which went bankrupt with debts of £100,000 – to John Manley, a gentleman of Milverton. Two years later he married the daughter of George Bacon of Harpford, whose memorial is in the south aisle of Langford Budville Church. From 1757 to 1849 members of the Webber-Haviland-Gardiner-Wade clan owned Bindon, either as occupiers or landlords. Their family names appear on plaques in the village church.

In 1838 the house was rented by Ernest Augustus Perceval, youngest son of twelve fathered by the one-time Solicitor General and Prime Minister Spencer Perceval. The Prime Minister has the dubious honour of being the only British PM to be murdered in office, when he was killed in the lobby of the House of Commons in 1812.

The Percevals' tenancy ended in 1849 and at the same time the estate was sold to Henry Moysey, a magistrate, for £6890 of 'lawful British money'. In 1857 an entrepreneur, John Hodges, converted Bindon into a private lunatic asylum, before selling it to Henry Warre in 1861.

Warre was born in Oporto of a family of wine merchants. He became a city stock-broker with strong local connections and left an indelible mark on the estate. As well as constructing the stables (now Bindon Home Farm), Bindon Cottage (built for his head gardener) and the house's west wing, he paid for an extension to the village church, now known as the Bindon Aisle, for the use of the household. At the time of the 1871 census there were 8 indoor servants, plus stable, garden and farm staff.

Henry's family crest and motto 'Je trouve bien' – ('I find well') - can been seen above the porch on Warre's west wing. He remained at Bindon until his death in 1875.

The census of 1881 shows the owner of the house to be Charles Lamport and family, proprietor of a prosperous shipbuilding firm employing 120 people. It was then that the Lamports radically altered the structure of the house. Rooms which dated from mediæval days disappeared to make way for the Great Hall, the stone staircase cited by John Trenchard was destroyed, replaced with teak, and an east wing, described as 'mixed Tudor' in style, was constructed. The east wing was later destroyed.

The Worthingtons were the next owners, acquiring the house in 1898. They were a wealthy Buckinghamshire family who used the house as a country retreat. Mrs. Worthington is said to have carved the lectern in St. Peter's Church, Langford Budville. In 1915 Captain, later Colonel, James Hamilton Leigh purchased Bindon and became the last owner of the entire Bindon Estate. After serving in the First World War in the Queen's own Cameron Highlanders, Colonel Leigh saw his investments lose their value and eventually retired to a small cottage in Banborough in the mid 1930's. Bindon was back on the market.

In 1934 it was advertised for auction. Clarence 'Gassie' Harris bought the house, which has since had a number of owners, including Basil Camden Prance (Mrs. Prance is remembered as an active W.I. member during the war years). The Augustinians of the Assumption used Bindon as a Noviciate and House of Studies from 1943 to 1950. After this there was a brief tenure with Horlicks Dairies and then the house stood empty and fell into disrepair. Fortuitously, Dr. James Hasson, a skin specialist who developed a cure for leprosy, acquired the house in 1961 and carried out extensive renovations. French born but a naturalised Englishman, he was physician to the Free French Forces in Britain during the war.

In 1981 Robert and Julia Small purchased the house and we are indebted to Julia for her very detailed study of the history of Bindon House. Julia Small wrote in 1985 – *The core of the house is 17th century, with 2 Georgian bow-fronts. 'Flemish' gables were added in the 1880s to match the height of a 'Jacobean' wing built at that time and later demolished in the mid-1930's. There is a mid-Victorian west wing with the crest of the builder above the pillared porch; an east/servants' annexe is probably c1830. The grounds contain a derelict cottage and a small bothy, a former conservatory and sports building called The Chapel, a dovecote and a 50ft greenhouse – the last about a hundred years old. The kitchen garden of nearly an acre is still walled on all sides.*

In 1996, when looking for a country house hotel in the area, Mark & Lynn Jaffa and their partners found their location at Bindon. After extensive renovations Bindon House was once again restored to its former glory and opened as a country house hotel and restaurant on 1st June 1997. Today the house stands in 7 acres of formal and woodland gardens. It has 12 en-suite rooms sleeping a total of 24 with the added facilities of an outdoor-heated swimming pool, tennis court, boules and croquet lawn. It is a 'Big House' to rent for family and friends, house party reunions and celebrations, weddings, shooting parties or conferences.

Bindon House today

The Old Vicarage *c1650*

The Old Church House with garden adjoining was church property until 1848 when Mr. Gidley, a church warden is said to have bought it. The style of the crook beams at the top of the building and the beams in the lower part of the building were crafted with axes rather than saws indicating that it was built between 1600-1650. The kitchen extension was added in 1860.

The Old Vicarage today

South Gundenham Farm

Sylvia Gothard

It is hard to pinpoint a date when the current house was built as no plans survive and innumerable alterations have been made or additions bolted on over the years though Gundenham Farm is documented as existing in 1615 when it was conveyed from Sir Nicholas Halswell and his son to Roger Bourne. The Haviland family acquired the Manor and Farm during the latter part of the 17th Century and continued in ownership until 1827. It was then sold to Edward Ayshford Sanford who held it until 1875. An affidavit to identify the property was obtained by the Sanford solicitors from one John Waygood who described himself as *aged ninety and upwards… and was employed as a labourer thereon for the space of fifty years.* Since 1928 three generations of the Gothard/ Cottrell family have farmed at South Gundenham. The valuation at that time appears to have changed little from the price paid to the Havilands a hundred years previously: low inflation or the state of agriculture at the time?

The farm has ranged from 70 to 180 acres over time although it has remained around 100 acres for the last hundred years. It was predominantly arable up to the late 19th Century when a move to milk and cheese production was made.

Spelling of the name has been inconsistent over the years with references to Gunham, Gunhamlands or even gonnham in various records. The manor may have taken its title from the Goundenham family who resided in the area around 1410 though under the Manerium de Langeford in the Lay Subsidy returns of 1327 are listed the names De Willelmo de Coundenham and Radulpho de Coundenham. An extract from "A

Somerset Coroners Roll 1315 – 1321" reads: *"Langford tithing: On 1 Jan 1317 William Corvyn of Langford found Henry le Schephurde of Bridport dead.* "The verdict at the inquest was that: *"Henry le Schephurde was in the service of William de Condenham. On 31 Dec 1316 he wanted to demolish a wall of an old house there with a pickaxe, but it fell on him and crushed him so that he died immediately by misadventure. The pickaxe is worth 2d for which Langford tithing will answer."* Among the jurors were William and Ralph de Condenham. Happily no sightings of ghostly pickaxe wielding medieval labourers have ever been reported.

On the other hand more tangible visitors to the farm have included several descendants of, or those with an interest in, previous owners, occupiers, neighbours or John Haviland the Philadelphia architect who was born here. They have come from as far afield as Germany, France, the United States and Australia. Apparently there is even a Gundenham House in Australia.

Philip Gothard has lived on the farm all his life, marrying Sylvia in 1973

Higher Ritherdons *c1750's*
A chocolate box thatched cottage which sadly burnt down in the late 50's. This was the demise of a number of thatched cottages in the village.

Photographed c1950

Croxhall *1908*

Apparently named after John Croxall, the former owner of the plot of land upon which it was built, this house was commissioned by the Sanford family, reputedly for the land agent of the Nynehead Estate. The first telephone in Langford Budville was installed here. The building originally had a flat roof, which was used for rainwater collection, but a pitched roof was added in the 1950s by the Fox family, who lived there for 60 years. In former times there had been stone quarry to the rear of the site, and a Bronze Age axe head was discovered there in 2007. A modern house, Quarry Leazes, was built in the grounds of Croxhall in 1989, when an Anglo-Saxon burial ground was unearthed.

Croxhall before the pitched roof was added

Public houses in Langford Budville
Martin Stockley

No doubt there have been public houses in Langford Budville for hundreds of years, helping to ease the thirst of its hard-working inhabitants. A licence to sell ale or beer has been required ever since the Alehouse Act of 1552, but for centuries it was the common drink of England for all classes of person and all ages, although in the West Country cider would also have been consumed in quantity. Low alcohol drinks like beer and cider were safer to consume than water, since there was less risk of contamination; they were drunk with most meals and provided a significant part of the population's required calorie intake.

Reference is made elsewhere in this book to the appearance of John Toogood, alehouse keeper of Langford Budville and Nicholas Ritherdon, probably another publican, before the Archdeacon's Court in 1624 for breaking the Sabbath. It has also been noted that the Church drew a significant amount of income from the sale of Church Ale during the week of the Revels. This was probably funded by the wealthier residents and the Churchwardens would use the donations to buy ale from local brewers or brew it themselves and sell it to the village revellers.

Later in the 17th century the Parsons family were alehouse keepers in the village and by the mid 18th century we can be fairly certain from the records of the Alehouse Keepers' Recognisance Rolls that there were 2 alehouses in Langford Budville. These records show the name of the innkeeper (who was not necessarily the owner of the property) and those of 2 other individuals providing sureties that the alehouse would be kept in an orderly fashion. From 1754 onwards there is a more or less continuous record of the landlords of Langford Budville's two public houses. They included Robert Waygood, William Hollard, John Dyer, John Thorn, Thomas and William Wood and William Pyne.

After 1775, the records show the names of these 2 pubs and reveal that at that time The New Inn was run by James Bear and the Rose and Crown by Thomas Martin. The Rose and Crown survives today as The Martlet.

The Martlet

The present day Martlet Inn is thought to be a 17th century stone and cob building; it was thatched until the 20th century. At one time the building and the land that went with it was known as Mill's tenement. There were certainly people named Mill in Langford Budville in earlier times, but whether they had a direct connection with this particular Mill's tenement, we do not know. As mentioned above, it seems to have been licensed premises since at least the mid 18th century and perhaps much earlier. The first known documented use of a name for the pub was The Rose and Crown in 1776, although within a couple of years the shortened form of 'The Crown' was being used. For the next hundred years the pub's name seems to have switched back and forth between 'The Rose and Crown' and 'The Crown'; perhaps 'The Crown' was the shorthand way it was always referred to locally. Various landlords came and went until, in 1796, Thomas Dinham took over and remained the licensee, and probably the owner, of The Crown for over 25 years.

In 1829 and again in 1831, John Dinham, who we take to be the son and inheritor of Thomas, raised a mortgage on the property and it is interesting to note that he went on later to become a licensed victualler in London. Meanwhile, however, a new licensee had arrived in 1823 named Ishmail Strong.

Thomas and John Dinham and their families are buried in St Peter's graveyard under the large memorial stones on the left as you enter the Church grounds. The Dinham family appear to have maintained a proprietary interest in the Rose and Crown until 1873, but the 1841 census lists the landlady as Sarah Flood. She lived there with her children Thomas, Jonathan, Joseph and Sarah, an elderly man named Thomas Brown – who may have been her father in law – and a servant girl named Charlotte Coombes. Sarah was presumably a widow and in 1846 she married William Miller, who was 10 years her junior, in Wellington and the two of them ran the pub for over 25 years. The (Rose and) Crown had farmland of around 50 acres attached to it in those days and William is described as a farmer, so it is likely that Sarah managed the licensed premises.

In 1873, the Sanfords acquired the Crown for the Nynehead Estate. A new landlord, Henry John Mills, took over and the pub changed its name to The Martlet, in reference to the Sanford coat of arms. However, by 1881 Henry Ousley and his wife Elizabeth, having previously been at the Hare and Hounds public house near Bindon (see below), were running the Martlet and did so until Henry died in 1895, when their daughter Annie took over for a few years. It is probably she who appears in the photograph.

In 1901 another long-term landlord took over and Fred Hancock was the licensee for a further 25 years. Since the late 1920s there have been at least 13 different landlords enjoying varying degrees of success. Villagers recall that the Martlet was closed for a year in the 1960s and that a landlord in the 1980s sold all the furniture and fittings before leaving under a cloud and causing the pub to go into receivership. Some major physical changes have taken place in recent years. In 2007 Vic and Paulette Bigg demolished the skittle alley and converted it into a function room, subsequently building a house behind the pub on what had been the garden and refurbishing the building alongside the Martlet to provide modern accommodation. Current owners Bruno Fellman and Terena Burgess have concentrated on the restaurant side of the business and built up a deserved reputation as one of the best eating places in the area. To accommodate the consequent increase in trade they have constructed a conservatory on the front of the building. However, The Martlet still welcomes its local drinkers and keeps an excellent pint of beer.

The Martlet c. 1900. Note that it was still thatched at this time.

The Martlet today – Bruno Fellman, Terena Burgess, Zeta the dog, Trevor and Betty Bloxham (Terena's mum)

Following refurbishment by Bruno and Terena, a party and blessing was held in Novenber 2009. This report is reproduced courtesy *Limited Edition* magazine. In addition to those named in the article, guests and staff in the photo top right are Harry Woods, Nina Vile, Lucy Morris, Amy Jennings, Emma Whittaker, Becci Hill, Josie Thomas
Wendy Thomas (photo bottom left) is also a Church Warden

Reopening party and bar blessing

Offical reopening of the refurbished Martlet Inn in Langford Budville

More than 100 guests of the Martlet Inn, Langford Budville, celebrated its official reopening and the blessing of the pub's bar in November.

In an unusual ceremony, the bar was blessed by the Father Russen Thomas from St Peter's Church in the village.

The pub has undergone two months of refurbishment and owners Bruno and Terena held a lavish party to honour the occasion.

Guests were treated to food, drink and music on the night.

The cosy village pub has always been popular with locals and visitors but Bruno and Terena, who bought the pub in July 2008, felt the bar and restaurant needed a revamp.

The couple, who previously ran The Seymour Arms in East Knoyle, have firmly established The Martlet as a favourite for anyone seeking great quality, locally sourced food.

Terena said: "We have always been proud of The Martlet and the service we offer, but we have now got it exactly as we want. The party is a way of showing off the pub and

thanking those who have supported us since our arrival."

The building work was carried out by local craftsmen Culverhay Builders.

■ Guests at the event.

■ Landlady Terena Burgess with Mac Latchy, Lynn Bailey, Barrie Taylor, Bill Seymour and Pam Hall.

■ Sandra Lawrence, Maggie Blake and Angie Gibbs.

■ John Harries, landlady Terena Burgess, Father Russen Thomas, landlord Bruno Fellman, Wendy Thomas and church warden Lyn Wyatt.

■ Alan Thomas and Ken Coles.

The New Inn

Returning to the 18th century, the reader may recall that there were two public houses in the village, one of which we have identified as today's Martlet. The other was situated in what is now called Old Post, up the road towards the Church from The Martlet. This was The New Inn. As with The Martlet (in those days The Rose and Crown or The Crown), The New Inn is first recorded by name in 1776, when the landlord was James Bear. Edward Giles took over in 1779 and six years later Agnes Tromlett became landlady for a further eight years. We then find William Phillips in charge for 27 years, from 1796 to 1822, and this period more or less coincides with Thomas Dinham's lengthy sojourn at the Crown. So Langford Budville had a long period of stability as far as its pubs were concerned.

By 1841 the census records Thomas Kerslake, aged 60, as an innkeeper in Langford Budville. The name of the pub is not stated in the census but a study of the tithing map shows that it was The New Inn, owned by a lady named Sarah Brown who also owned adjacent land and property. Thomas Kerslake lived in The New Inn with his younger wife Elizabeth and their two children. Unfortunately the Kerslakes have vanished by the time of the 1851 census and there is no further reference to The New Inn until 1891, when it seems to have become the name of a dwelling house rather than a working pub, as it is occupied by a carpenter and his family.

There was a family named Sully living in Langford Budville in 1851, in which William Sully is described as a chairmaker and his wife as an innkeeper. Whether they occupied and ran The New Inn, or some other unidentified licensed premises, we have not yet been able to discover, but in any case by 1861 they had taken over a pub in North Street, Wellington and it seems The New Inn had finally called time for ever.

The Hare and Hounds

In 1830 Parliament passed the Beerhouse Act which enabled anybody to brew and sell beer on payment of a licence fee of 2 guineas. This very liberal law was aimed partly at weaning the public off the consumption of cheap gin, which had grown enormously in the previous hundred years and by general consensus was now causing all manner of social problems. Unsurprisingly therefore, we find that by the time of the 1841 census the number of public houses in Langford Budville had risen beyond the two long-established premises of The Crown and The New Inn. One such new arrival was the Hare and Hounds, which was part of the Bindon House estate. It was in an old stone cottage that still stands behind the more recently constructed lodge house on the north side of the drive to Bindon House as it meets the Wiveliscombe road.

William and Margaret Richards ran the Hare and Hounds in 1841 and lived there with their son and four daughters. Ten years later it appears that the son (also named William) had married and taken over the running of the pub. His wife Elizabeth was 28 at the time, but she was soon to be widowed, leaving her in sole charge of the Hare and Hounds and caring for her four young children. In 1864 Elizabeth remarried; her new husband was Henry Ousley and he obtained work as a gardener on the estate. Together they ran the Hare and Hounds and with them lived Elizabeth's four children by her first marriage, together with young Annie Ousley who was a product of this second marriage. However, by 1881 the Hare and Hounds was no more and the cottage was occupied by an agricultural labourer and his wife. The Ousleys had taken over the Martlet (see above).

Doorway of Old Inn formerly The Hare and Hounds

Other Licensed Premises

Apart from the Sullys (see The New Inn, above) whose precise location is not absolutely certain, one other licensed victualler appears in 19th century Langford Budville. In 1841, Thomas Delbridge is described as an innkeeper, aged 60. He lived with what were presumably his wife Dorothy, 75, and a William Delbridge who may have been a grandson as he was only 18 years old. It is difficult to be absolutely sure of the location of these premises but the 1843 tithe map shows that Thomas Delbridge owned and occupied 2 cottages with gardens opposite the top of Chorwell Lane (approximately where the Working Men's Club once stood and where there is now a car park for Reynolds and a modern house called Treetops). So there was probably a public house on that site for a short while in the middle of the 19th century.

Approximate dateline for buildings in Langford Budville

Year	*House*
Pre 1600	Ritherdons Stancombe
Pre 1700	Bindon House Gundenham Martlet Old Forge c1602 Old Vicarage c1650 Hillview Poor House
Pre 1800	Old Post St. Peter's Cottage Brockney House Higher Ritherdons
Pre 1900	Rose Cottages Sunnyside & SunnyView 1850 Springwood 1865 Chy-an-mor 1890 Shattocks Cottages The Old Chapel Butts Coneybeare
Pre 1950	Croxhall c1908 Myrtle, Rose, Heathfield etc Cottages 1908 *(Myrtle Cottage built by John Twyford for £190 2s. 0d)* Bindon Lodge c1910 Oddmeads c 1911 Reynolds, Sunnyside & Field View 1926 Chapel View 1 & 2 1939 White Oaks 1940-50
Pre 2000	1 Ritherdons, Orchard Corner, 3 Higher Ritherdons, Miles Green plus bungalows from Martlet Car Park upwards 1950-60 Yew Tree 1958 Little Pippins, The Fiddlers, Wayside, Strathmartine, Hawthorne 1960's Swifts 1964 – built on former allotments Coppins, The Wedge 1965 Meadowside & Greenlands – 1968-70 Tranquila 1971 Sliema, Annondale & Newstead 1976 Treetops, Orchards & Petersmead 1978
Pre 2010	Little Acorns, Crownfield houses facing Martlet 1982 Quarry Leazes 1988 (riginally Fairlawn) Elderberry House 1995 The Willows 1999 Orchard Cottage 2000 Courtlands development 2008

Chapter 7 – **CHURCH & CHAPEL**

The Church of St Peter
M. B. McDermott

Foreword

Research into the ecclesiastical history of Langford Budville has been complicated by two special factors: the disappearance of most of the earlier records of the archdeaconry of Taunton, and Langford Budville's status, until 1863, as a chapelry of Milverton. This has made it impossible to compile a complete and wholly reliable list of curates, for instance. On the other hand, the parish registers and churchwardens' accounts survive from the mid-sixteenth century in an almost unbroken series, and these have proved an invaluable source of historical information. Where the dates quoted in this booklet have been drawn from the churchwardens' accounts, these denote an administrative year which began during the previous calendar year.

Of the many other sources which have been used, mention should be made here of N. Pevsner's *The Buildings of England: South and West Somerset* and of the notebooks of the Rev. S. J. Swainson. Further reference may be made to the fully annotated versions of this booklet which have been deposited with the vicar of Langford Budville and with the Somerset Archaeological Society in Taunton.

The writer alone must bear the responsibility for any errors contained in this booklet, but he wishes to acknowledge with gratitude the help and advice given by the Rev. P. R. Scott, Mr. T. J. Hunt, Dr. R. W. Dunning, and the staff of the Somerset Record Office, and also the assistance given by Marjorie Stockley and Christopher Fox in the preparation of the 2011 edition.

Introduction

The parish of Langford Budville lies mid-way between Wellington and Milverton, and the church, which is constructed of local red sandstone and conglomerate, with honey-coloured Hamstone windows and other dressed features, is composed of a nave, side aisles, chancel (with combined vestry and organ-chamber on the north side) and a three-storeyed west tower. The tower may appear rather plain in comparison with the finest in the county but is nevertheless an impressive structure, and the church as a whole makes a very pleasing visual impression which is heightened by its hill-top position: for the building stands as a landmark in the surrounding landscape, with the tower dominating the village below, and from it there are magnificent views of the Brendon and Quantock Hills, the Vale of Taunton Deane and the Blackdowns, whilst Sedgemoor and even the Poldens are visible on a clear day.

The Medieval Manor and Chapelry

The Somerset manor of 'Langeford', held by Godwin, son of Harold, in 1066 but by William the Conqueror at the time of Domesday Book in 1086, may refer to Langford in Burrington (in North Somerset) but recent historical opinion has identified this manor with Langford Budville. The suffix 'Budville' refers to the de Budville family which held the manor by 1212 and for a time subsequently.

Langford Budville had a church by 1204, but this was a chapelry of Milverton and did not become a parish church until 1863. The precise date of the foundation of the chapelry is not known, but a chaplain named Nicholas Bagga is recorded as a witness to a grant of land made by Roger Arundel to the monks of Canonsleigh, Devon, at some time before 1204. In c.1989 a group of burials was discovered in a garden to the south of the church on the opposite side of the road. If, as has been suggested, these burials are of Saxon date, this might suggest a pre-Conquest date for the foundation of the church, although this is difficult to reconcile with the fact that the present medieval building is separated from the burials by an apparently long-established road. Conceivably the burials represent an overspill cemetery, perhaps associated with famine and plague in the 14th century.

In 1241 the church of Milverton (with its chapelry in Langford Budville) was granted by Bishop Jocelin to the archdeacon of Taunton who thereafter derived income from the parish and appointed a vicar to undertake pastoral responsibilities, assisted, on occasions at least, by a chaplain or curate serving in Langford Budville.

In 1242/3 there was an enquiry into the death of "Nicholas the chaplain of Langeford" whose body was found at Burdon (possibly Burn Hill on the road to Milverton) where he had fallen from his horse. Nicholas' successor was a chaplain named Robert, who is mentioned in 1243, but the next known reference to a chaplain is not until 1381, when Richard Puryman was reported to Chancery for non-payment of taxes. It is possible that there were periods of time during the middle ages when Langford was not, in fact, provided with its own curate, and this may be implied by the fact that in 1351 the rector of Runnington was given permission by Bishop Ralph to celebrate mass every day in the chapel of Langford Budville. This arrangement may have been made to fill a gap created by the Black Death, which killed a number of Somerset clergy.

Architecture

The architectural style of the present church building is Perpendicular and therefore late medieval in period (with the exception of the Victorian north aisle and vestry). The appearance of the building in Nicholas Bagga's time remains a matter of speculation, however, for the first documentary reference to the fabric is dated 1509. In that year John Peryn of Wellington bequeathed 3/4d "to the fabric of the new tower of the parish church of Longford", and it is possible that this indicates not only the age of the present tower but the approximate date of the rebuilding or alteration in Perpendicular style of the church as a whole, for the way in which the west end of the south aisle embraces one of the tower buttresses suggests that the aisle in its present form cannot pre-date the tower. The four three-light Perpendicular windows of this aisle appear to be identical in design (type III according to Pevsner's classification), but the intrusion of a piscina into one of the sills implies the existence of an earlier aisle (or south transept) which was subjected to drastic alteration when the windows were inserted.

There are strong similarities between the east window in the chancel, the west window in the tower and the western window in the north wall of the north aisle. These also are three-light Perpendicular windows (type II). The second window in the north wall of the latter aisle is exceptional in that it has four lights, but it is still typically Perpendicular: more will be said later about the presence of such windows in this Victorian addition to the church.

The south arcade has typical Somerset piers of the late-medieval period (type A, with hollows in the diagonals) except that the four attached shafts of each pier do not have individual capitals: instead, each capital is in the form of an encircling band around the top of the pier. The decorative carving on these bands may represent foliage, but lace-work has also been suggested – particularly in the case of the eastern pier which also incorporates a carved needle-and-thread. This pier is elongated to form a double respond in which the capitals of the two responds are set at different heights to correspond with the differing floor levels within the church. The double respond may indicate that there was a projecting side chapel or transept before the south aisle was built, or it may have been intended to provide extra strength to support the thrust from the chancel arch.

The exact significance of the Langford Needle is not clear. It may merely have been a mason's invention, but two rather more elaborate theories have been put forward. A needle and thread motif is associated with Queen's College, Oxford, and it has been suggested that Dr. John Caldebek. a former fellow of Queen's who was vicar of Wellington from 1465 to 1498, may have played a part in the late-medieval rebuilding of Langford church. The alternative view is that the needle and thread carving indicates that a woman provided the necessary patronage, and a link with Canonsleigh Abbey has been suggested. On the central boss of the wagon roof of the south aisle is a shield bearing three chevronels and this is repeated on the north side of that roof and again on the south side of the wagon roof of the nave: no colouring survives, but the form coincides with the arms of Matilda de Clare who re-founded Canonsleigh Abbey as a house of Augustinian canonesses in 1284. The roof bosses were re-carved in the nineteenth century, however, and their authenticity is therefore open to some doubt.

The Reformation

In the 1548 Survey of Chantries it was reported that a light which was supposed to be kept burning perpetually within the church had fallen into disuse at least ten years previously, despite an endowment of rent from a property in Milverton. The Survey was made early in the reign of Edward V1, and during the following years the local congregation experienced the impact of the Reformation. In 1550 the churchwardens purchased a communion book (presumably a reference to Cranmer's First Prayer Book) and sold to Thomas Pery a painted cloth which hung before the rood loft: the latter would have surmounted a rood screen at the junction of the chancel and the nave.

In the following year the rood loft itself was dismantled and the "pictures" (or painted figures?) of Mary and John, which would have been placed on either side of the rood (crucifix), were sold to John Phelyps for 3d. The ornamental panels of the ceilure above the position of the rood screen still survive.

In 1551 the side altar was removed from the east end of the south aisle where its position is indicated by the survival of a piscina and the remains of a ceilure. There is a second piscina in the south wall of the chancel beside what was originally the high altar, and the outlets from both piscinas were at one time visible near ground level in the outer faces of the walls.

Mary Tudor

During the reign of Mary Tudor there occurred a short-lived return to the old faith, and this is reflected in the fact that in 1557 John Wallrond's wife made a gift of a mass book to the church, whilst the churchwardens purchased a tabernacle (to contain the eucharistic elements associated with the mass) and a palm-cross: the latter would have been used in the revived Palm Sunday celebrations. The accounts for 1557 also refer to the moving of the holy water stoup: there was additional expense for plastering the aisle in this connection, and the stoup can still be seen embedded in the wall of the south aisle immediately to the east of the door. The stoup was presumably moved from outside the south door, and it is possible that this alteration provides a date for the building of the porch – for the presence of an empty niche over the inner door (a niche whose canopy, moreover, has been mutilated to make room for the porch ceiling) indicates that the porch was erected at a later date than the south aisle.

The rood loft must also have been restored at some time, for there is a reference to its being repaired and painted in 1575; and the screen itself may have survived until 1808 when there is a reference to "taking down the Screen in the Church".

The Langford Revel

The problem of raising funds for the church is by no means a new one, and a normal method employed in the sixteenth century involved the brewing of ale which was sold at a parish festivity named, like the beer itself, a "church ale". Church ales often took place, in the West Country at least, in a building known as a Church House (a good example of which still survives in the village of Crowcombe), although the nave of the church itself had originally been used. In Langford Budville the annual festivity was known as the Langford Revel: this took place at the festival of St. Peter. and the ale which the churchwardens were responsible for brewing was known as "St. Peter's ale". There was a Church House in the village (on the site of the private garden to the south-west of the churchyard) at least as early as 1551, and it is significant that although the churchwardens let a room in the building to the rector of Runnington to use as a school in 1620, they still reserved the use of the property to themselves for a fortnight every year "to sell there parish ale".

The Langford Revel was eventually suppressed during the Interregnum, and the puritans' hostility towards revels in general is perhaps made more understandable by the fact that the Langford tythingman (constable) and his assistants, who had the task of enforcing the prohibition, were abused and beaten up by a crowd of young men from Wellington who had come "to keepe revel" on the village green where they were "strikinge each at the other with staffs, whoopinge and makeinge a greate disturbance"! The Revel was later revived. but was finally brought to an end in the mid-nineteenth century after further outbreaks of violence had occurred. Langford Church House, on the other hand, was converted into a parish poor-house after 1650, and eventually passed into private ownership in (probably) the 1830s: the building was burnt down in 1908.

The Seventeenth Century

In 1614 the churchwardens purchased an hour glass "for the preacher". but this seems to have become somewhat of an irrelevance by 1623, however, for in that year Thomas Wygood (or Wigwood), the curate was rebuked by the archdeacon's court for not giving the required monthly sermons! During the years leading up to the Civil War, a number of visiting preachers entered the parish, and from 1636 they were expected to sign a register kept by the churchwardens. Wygood, who eventually died in 1640 at the age of one hundred, was also reprimanded in 1623 for failing to catechize the children of Langford Budville, and the churchwardens were indicted for not providing a "decent and comly pulpitt cloth". The records of the archdeacon's court only survive for 1623/4, but even in that short period there are numerous other references to Langford Budville: John Fursdon and his wife, for instance, were "vehemently suspected to be recusants refusing to come to the church on the Sabbath day", whilst a number of parishioners were indicted for having been "in the house of John Toogood on the Saboth daie typling and drinking at the time of divine service".

After the execution of Charles I the royal coat of arms, which had been set up (possibly over the chancel arch) in 1608, was defaced; and William Jewell, who was Wygood's successor as curate, appears to have been expelled, for the registers ceased to be written in Jewell's own immaculate hand and the parishioners then "subscribed for a minister". In 1660, however, both King and Church of England were restored, and the churchwardens subsequently set up a new royal coat of arms in the church.

In 1663 the inhabitants of Langford Budville complained to the archdeacon of Taunton that the village "for divers yeares past hath byn destitute of a residing minister", and they petitioned him to appoint William Crofts as vicar in his own right (as opposed to being a mere chaplain) for a period of twenty-one years. This request may well have been granted, for Crofts' signature, with the style "vicar", appears in the registers in the later 1660s, and he was described as "vicar of this parrish" when buried in 1675. Crofts' successor, Nicholas Comer, may have inherited this vicarial status, for he also occasionally used the term "vicar" with reference to himself. There is clear evidence, however, that Langford was once again recognized as a chapelry of Milverton during the eighteenth century.

Church Music

At an unspecified date a gallery was installed in the church. The first reference to this structure is dated 1742, and the fact that there was a "gallery window" may suggest that the gallery itself was built under the tower where it would be lit by the west window. The probable purpose of this gallery was to provide accommodation for the church musicians and choir, for there are references in the later eighteenth century to "teaching the Singers" and to the purchase of a "Singing Book full of Tunes", whilst the musical accompaniment was provided by a village band which included bass and treble viols. In 1838, however, a barrel organ was installed in the church. The present organ was built by Forster and Andrews of Hull in 1875 (cf. Burlescombe church), and presumably replaced the organ referred to in 1873 as having been lent by Edward Ayshford Sanford and originally from Chipley Park. These changes probably provide an approximate date for the dismantling of the gallery.

Another aspect of the organization of the church services is the fact that Langford Budville seems to have conformed to the usual custom of segregating the sexes. As early as 1550 there is a reference to a payment being made to the churchwardens for a seat for three women, and the position of some of the seats for women is indicated by a reference in 1735 to "new making 20 womens seats through-out the Back part of the Middle Isle of the Church".

Victorian Alterations

With the coming of the Victorian era there was a revival of interest in the fabric of the church. Thus the accounts for 1846 included heavy expenditure on "the re-seating and thorough repair of the Parish Church", and in 1847 it was decided to raise money for the building of a new aisle. The latter plan was in fact dropped, but the north aisle (the Bindon Aisle) was eventually built by Henry Warre of Bindon House in 1866: it was originally intended for the exclusive use of the Bindon household, but Warre agreed to allow five seats for the use of other parishioners. The architect was John Hayward of Exeter.

In connection with the earlier plan to build a north aisle, the mason was instructed to re-use the two windows (of three and four lights respectively) in the north wall of the nave, and this is evidently what happened in 1866. Faculty plans of the existing layout in 1866 and of the proposed new aisle show a pair of three- and four-light windows in the north wall in each case, and examination of the present windows confirms their authenticity, especially when compared with the 'mock Gothic' window inserted in the west end of the aisle, for their tracery is true to Somerset Perpendicular type, the external stonework is weathered and the outer edges of the external jamb-stones are irregular.

The building of the Bindon Aisle was the occasion on which the stairway to the rood loft was destroyed, for the stairway was referred to in 1862 and one of the plans of 1866 shows a small turret, which would have contained the stairway, at the east end of the north wall of the nave prior to the construction of the aisle.

Another feature of the church which was referred to in 1862 was "the chancel arch, which fits exactly into the roof of the chancel". The present arch must have been erected soon after this, but the earlier high arch, with its carved imposts, can still be seen on the east side. The vestry and organ chamber date from 1873 when their construction was approved by the Rev. T.H. Sotheby (a considerable benefactor to the church) at a vestry meeting at which he found himself the only person present!

When the porch of the National School (which was originally built in 1851) was being dismantled in 1928, the stone-work, which was identified by a mason as coming from Hele, showed traces of "conventional stalked leaf foliage", although this carved work was subsequently hidden from view when the porch was rebuilt. The piers on either side of the entrance to the school playground and the gateway to Langford Court (which was used as a curate's residence in the 1850s) also appear to be constructed of this type of stone (probably North Curry sandstone which was quarried at Hele) and it is possible that all these features are relics of stonework discarded from the church during the Victorian alterations. The "stalked leaf foliage" is suggestive of the Early English style of the late 12th or 13th centuries, which would correspond with the earliest documentary evidence of the existence of the church.

Parish Status

The alterations to the fabric of the church which occurred during the Victorian period were accompanied by a significant development of another kind. Langford Budville's long-standing dependence upon Milverton is emphasized by the 1841 tithe map which describes the vicar of Milverton, the Rev. John Thomas Trevelyan, as the owner of the glebe in Langford. In contrast, the Rev. Robert Campbell (who in 1841 was living in the former Church House) is merely styled "resident curate" in a printed version of the farewell sermon which he preached at Langford church in September 1842. In 1863, however, Langford Budville finally lost its subordinate position as a chapelry and was granted the status of a perpetual curacy separate from Milverton, although the archdeacon of Taunton remained the patron of the living. Perhaps as a measure of this new-found status, a new vicarage, now known as Springwood was then built on the site known as Coneybear which was obtained in 1865 from Mr. E. A. Sanford (the lord of the manor) in exchange for the old thatched "vicarage"(strictly speaking this had only been a curate's house) and the church land on which it stood. The latter building, which may date from the late seventeenth century when an earlier structure was demolished, was described in 1815 as "a poor thatched cottage... unfit for the Residence of a Clergyman". Mention has already been made of the use of the former Church House and of Ritherdons House (now Langford Court) as substitute accommodation during the 1840s and 1850s respectively. In c.1970 a new vicarage was built in the grounds of its Victorian predecessor, but this vicarage has in its turn become a private residence and Langford Budville is now served by a non-resident team vicar.

Union with Runnington

A further change, which was decreed by an Order in Council issued in 1930, was the uniting of Langford Budville with the neighbouring parish of Runnington. This came into effect in 1932 when the Rev. S. J. Swainson became the first incumbent to hold the united benefice.

The Exterior

The overall external appearance of the church has already been mentioned, but there are a number of details which merit attention, including the priest's door in the south wall of the chancel and the base of the old churchyard cross immediately to the south-east of the porch. The buttress built against the south aisle is a late addition and is associated with a wooden beam placed across the interior of the aisle to support one of the piers of the south arcade. There are empty niches over both the inner and outer doorways of the porch, which is also mounted by two carved stone beasts (possibly an eagle and a leopard) on its outer corners, and the porch and south aisle carry pinnacled parapets with quatrefoils: certain of the latter appear to frame the crossed keys of St. Peter, although it has been claimed that the church was originally dedicated to St. James. The carved heads at the stops of the hood-mouldings of the windows of the south aisle may be later re-cuts, and it has been suggested that they represent the seven deadly sins. The churchyard at one time housed the village stocks, which were still in existence in 1873. The lower churchyard, however, is an addition which was consecrated in 1875.

The Tower

The tower has battlements and a stair-turret on the south-east corner, and is supported by set-back buttresses. The Langford Revel included a custom known as "clipping the tower" in which a human chain was formed around the church: a ritual dance was then performed, and at a given moment in the proceedings a shout was raised and the devil was chased out of the churchyard as far as the River Tone at Harpford.

The Bells

The clock on the west face of the tower was presented by the Rev. T. H. Sotheby in 1881, and there is a peal of six bells within the tower. The oldest original bells bear the dates 1687 and 1738, the latter bell having been cast by Thomas Wroth of Wellington. Two of the other bells were made respectively by Thomas Bilbie of Cullompton in 1810 and Gillett & Co. of Croydon in 1885, the latter being a further gift of the Rev. T.H. Sotheby. Llewellins & James of Bristol recast a tenor bell of 1600 (originally made by George Purdue of Taunton) in 1896, and also a bell of 1663 (by John Pennington) in 1904.

In 1992 the bells were retuned at the Whitechapel Bell Foundry, but the tenor bell of 1896, which required recasting, was replaced by the redundant 7th bell from St Saviour's Church, Lark Hall, Bath, which was cast by I. Rudhall in 1830. At the same time a new steel bell frame was installed in the ringers' chamber so that the defective wooden frame dating from 1753 could be preserved in the belfry. A new ringers' gallery was constructed behind the tower arch and a glass screen inserted between the gallery and the nave. John Matthews led the fund-raising for this expensive project, Robert Parker was in charge of handling and reinstalling the bells and of designing and making the steel bell frame, and Ray Arscott was responsible for the joinery, including the new ringers' gallery.

The Interior

Monuments

The church possesses a number of monuments. On the north wall of the chancel, for instance, is a memorial (by Thomas King of Bath) to William Barry Wade of Bindon

The interior of the Church looking East

House (d. 1806) in the form of a marble oval with two figures in relief on either side of an urn, and on either side of the east window of the south aisle are memorials to William Bacon (d. 1663) and to Capt. George Bacon of Harpford (d. 1690): the latter monuments are flanked by pillars with ionic capitals and surmounted by broken pediments framing the family arms.

Windows

The painted windows in the chancel and tower were presented by the Rev. Sotheby, whilst the two windows in the Bindon Aisle were presented in memory of Henry Warre (d. 1875) by his sons Francis and Edmund. The window to the west of the porch was inserted in memory of John Lamont of Benmore (d. 1850), and the east window of the south aisle was given in memory of John de Haviland, "Inventor of Radiating prisons", who was born at Gundenham in 1792 and died in 1852, by his son John.

Memorial to Capt. George Bacon

The Font

The octagonal font is Perpendicular in design, and the blank face on one side of the Hamstone bowl indicates that it was designed to stand against a wall, possibly near the door. The stem is very ornate, but it does not appear to be carved from identical stone to that of the bowl, and it is doubtful whether there is sufficient space underneath the bowl for the missing points of the corner pinnacles: it is therefore questionable whether the bowl and stem are an original combination.

The Church Plate

The oldest piece of church plate is a silver Elizabethan communion cup which is still occasionally used in the communion service: the cover bears the date 1573, which indicates that the cup was purchased in accordance with a contemporary order that pre-Reformation chalices (associated with the mass) were to be replaced. Another item of church plate is a silver dish with a wide brim: this has been dated by its hallmarks to the reign of Charles II (but not later than 1678), and bears the arms of Edward Clarke of Chipley and his wife Mary Jepp. The church also possesses a chalice, paten and flagon, each made of silver (with the date letter for 1848) and inscribed with the initials of Edward Ayshford Sanford and the date 1866.

The Parish Bier

There is evidence that a bier was in use at funerals in Langford during the seventeenth century. The last example of such a vehicle in the parish was purchased in c.1929 and, after many years of disuse, finally sold in 1970.

Curates of Langford Budville

The following list is based on the known references to chaplains or curates who appear to have been appointed to serve the chapelry of Langford Budville as such. There are bound to be omissions, although the petition of 1663 indicates that Langford was not always provided with its own curate. Roger Person and William Persone, who are mentioned in 1481 and 1557 respectively, are unlikely to have been "parsons" and are therefore excluded from the list. The dates prior to 1793 do not necessarily denote the year of each curate's appointment.

Before 1204:   Nicholas Bagga.
   1242/3:   Nicholas.
   1243:   Robert.
   1381:   Richard Puryman.

1410: John Loveney.
1594: William More.
1598: Thomas Wigwood.
1640: William Jewell. Possibly assistant to Wigwood from 1633.
1650: The parishioners subscribed for a minister after Jewell's (presumed) expulsion.
1660: John Wigwood. Described as "Clarke" when buried in that year: it is not clear whether he was a curate who had served in Langford Budville.
1663: William Crofts.
1675: Nicholas Comer. Signed the registers until 1701.
1727: Thomas Evans. Signed the registers until 1746.
1784: Thomas Hopkins.
1793: James Randolph. Received a stipend of £30.
1805: Charles Henry Sampson, B.A.
1832: Robert Allan Scott, M.A. Received a stipend of £60.
1832: Richard Robert Campbell. Farewell sermon: 1842.
1844: Richard Burridge, B.A. Received a stipend of £100.
1844: Henry Folkes Edgell, B.A.
1849: Harvey Alexander, B.A. He was appointed as a curate in Milverton in 1847, but appears to have replaced Edgell in Langford Budville in 1849.
1855: William H. Walrond. There is no record of his being licensed, but he signed the registers from 1855.

Perpetual Curates

1863: William H. Walrond.
1866: William Henry Fowle, B.A.
1868: Thomas Hans Sotheby, B.A. (until 1888).
1883: Francis William Raban, B.A. (assistant curate).
1887: Thomas Buncombe (assistant curate).
1888: W. H. Fowle (again).
1894: Charles Henry Luxton, B.A.
1919: Samuel James Swainson, M.A.
1949: David Cuthbert Mercier, M.A.
1955: William Lincoln Jones, B.A.
1961: Perceval Roy Scott, R.N.
1974: Howard Charles Campbell Bowen, B.A.
1980: Charles Edward Rolfe.
1986: Andrew Gidleigh Bruce Rowe, A.K.C., R.N.
1995: David Peter Randall, B.A.
2005: Interregnum.
2006: Margi Campbell, B.A.
2012: Alan Ellacott

The Gospel Hall – affectionately known in later years as The Chapel

The catalyst for this book was this photograph of the 1916 Anniversary Group which Sarah Nutt had been given when she bought her house now called The Old Chapel. It began the search for more old photographs and information about the village. Sadly we have not been able to name any of the people in the photograph but we live in hope.

Butts Cottages c1900

In 1870 Gospel meetings were being held at Butts Cottages in the house where in later years William and Hilda Harris lived. (Hilda was caretaker of the Working Men's Club for many years). They were conducted by Mr Cuff, who was connected to the

Congregational Church, and who was followed by a Mr. Webb and a Mr. Lemon. In 1870 Mr Passmore, connected with the Millway Assembly in Wellington, undertook 'the work'. In 1881, at the request of the parishioners, a Sunday School was started with Mr. J. Bowerman as the first superintendent, followed by Mr. S. Bowerman. Over the years attendance increased and so a new place was sought. Mr. Charles Lamport of Bindon House was approached and he agreed in 1893 to sell them a cottage which was at that time used as a laundry, to be a place of worship (now The Old Chapel). An independent trust was then formed for the purpose of continuing evangelical work in the village. The mortgage for the building was paid off in 1936 and a thanksgiving service was held to commemorate the occasion. In the 1930's a Mr Charles Bowyer succeeded Mr S Bowerman as Superintendent and remained in the post until his death in 1961, after which his son Clifford continued to run the Chapel and Sunday School.

Betty Sparks & Mr & Mrs Charles Bowyer

Janet Read (née Brewer) and Valerie Pitman (née Brewer) outside the Gospel Hall c1958.

There was clearly, at times, some conflict with the parish Church of St Peter, although this seems to have been resolved in later years (see the Parish Magazine article below). The Rev S J Swainson (vicar of St Peter's 1919-1949) noted in his Record of Church Life and Affairs that his predecessor Rev Fowle (1888-1894) *"did not have a good time in his day, as the Plymouth Brethren Chapel was built."* Rev Swainson goes on to observe that *"In 1938 Sunday School numbers* [for St Peter's] *decreased – the inducements offered by the other place of worship increased"* and that although *"In 1940 an influx of refugees led to growth of the* [St Peters'] *Sunday School to 34 at Langford and 24 at Runnington,...the other place of worship intensified their efforts and gifts."*

Among the inducements offered were various celebratory events throughout the year, for which the Working Men's Club and the owners of the gardens at Oddmeads generously provided venues. The Wellington Weekly News reported on the annual Gospel Hall Sunday School treat in June 1934, held in the grounds of Oddmeads courtesy of the owner, Mr Ash. After lunch there were all manner of games for the children to enjoy and the adults to watch, until a 4.00 o'clock gong announced afternoon tea for the children. This was followed by a tea for the adults – to which about 60 sat down, so the function was clearly well attended. After some short speeches, more fun and games ensued until the tired children were called together at around 8.30pm to give *"3 hearty cheers"* to the organisers, and the proceedings closed with the singing of the Doxology.

By the 1980's attendance at both the Sunday School and evening services had fallen back significantly, so the Trustees, in conjunction with the Charity Commission, agreed to close the Chapel and put the property on the market. The proceeds of the subsequent sale were divided equally between St. Peter's Church, the Langford Budville Village Hall Project and Mullers Children's Orphanage in Bristol. A plaque in the Church commemorates this gift.

From the Langford Budville Parish Magazine – April 1970

Nearly 90 years ago a horse and trap could have been seen coming down the hill at Ritherdons bringing the washing from Bindon House, occupied then by the Lamport family of the old Shipping Line of Lamport & Holt, to their laundry in the Village.

Through the march of progress this building, which was also the residence of the laundress and her family, became redundant. At this time a group of Taunton business men, led by Mr. Robert Hatcher, founder of the famous high street departmental stores, were building or adapting premises in some of the villages in this area as Chapels. So 82 years ago the two storey laundry and house was converted into a Chapel by removing most of the upper floor. The first service held in the small upstairs room was conducted by Mr. Thomas Penny of the Taunton Timber firm. Annually in early June this event is commemorated by anniversary services, as is the custom in most Chapels in the Spring and early Summer.

Since then without a break, except for bad weather, local preachers or laymen of various denominations and occupations have come on foot, by pony and trap, by bicycle and present day form of motorised transport. The most hectic journey ever experienced by some members of the congregation from Wellington was on the night of the famous January 1929 gale. During the service the soft Tracebridge slates were doing flying saucer acts. Afterwards they had to crawl under and over the trunks and through the branches of the many trees that were across the roads, including 6 large elms at the top of Gundenham Lane which came down side by side like ninepins.

The small wrought iron entrance gate is the work of the illustrious and well loved village blacksmith, Mr. Charlie Wood. This is a memorial to his keen interest and support for the Chapel over half a century. Except for illness he sat Sunday by Sunday in the back seat by the coke stove with members of his family. One can remember and fancy that they can almost hear the sound of his wheelbarrow, filled with fruit and vegetables, on the Saturday afternoon before the Harvest Festival.

We are most grateful to the Rev. P.R. Scott for this privilege of contributing to the Parish Magazine. Also we are most thankful that there is such a happy spirit of understanding and cooperation between those who worship at the Parish Church and those at the Chapel, which came into being during the ministry of the Rev. D. Mercier – 1949-1955.

The Church in Recent Times

Throughout the years the village as a whole has continued generously to support fundraising events in order to maintain the church. For example in 1992 a large group of sponsored cyclists rode from Langford Budville to Wells to raise money to re-tune and re-hang the church bells. In the last few years the church has been filled for concerts organised by long-term church warden Mike Sertin, featuring Top Brass, a musical brass ensemble, and in 2009 Laurian Cooper invited actress Cleo Sylvestre to portray 'Mary Seacole' - a professional 'first' for the village.

Since the Reverend Margi Campbell left the parish in 2011 the village has been without a vicar. Father Russen Thomas, together with lay reader Sandra Lee and an occasional church service taken by the Reverend Josie Harrison, have kept the spiritual wheels turning. A new team vicar, the Reverend Alan Ellacott, will be taking over the reins on 4th July and everyone is looking forward to welcoming him to what will be another phase in the Church's long history.

St Peter's continues to play an important and active role in village life. Current church wardens Lyn Wyatt and Wendy Thomas, together with the Parochial Church Council and members of the church, organise a number of traditional fund-raising events throughout the year (Plant sale, Proms in the Park, Christmas Fair, Harvest lunch etc.) as well as all the church festivals and services,

St Peter's is extremely lucky to play host to the Langford Budville Bell-ringers, who practise weekly as well as ring for special occasions. They are a very successful team under the leadership of John Hill and Jean Mathison and have won a number of prizes for expert ringing.

It is hoped that the Church will continue to play an important role in village life and not suffer the fate of so many beautiful Somerset churches – closure due to lack of support.

Bell Ringing – Friends Open Day 2nd April 2011

Friends of St. Peter's Church

This scheme was launched in 2009 to allow people who do not necessarily attend the Church the opportunity to help preserve the fabric of the building by giving financially or in kind. Since its inception the group has been in receipt of generous bequests and has also organised Christmas Tree Lighting-Up Ceremonies, an Open Day, the refurbishment and painting of the Church Porch, a performance in the Church of *Under Milk Wood* by Dylan Thomas and a Spring Garden Party in the grounds of Langford Court courtesy of Richard and Jane Lloyd. To date the scheme has raised in excess of £3000

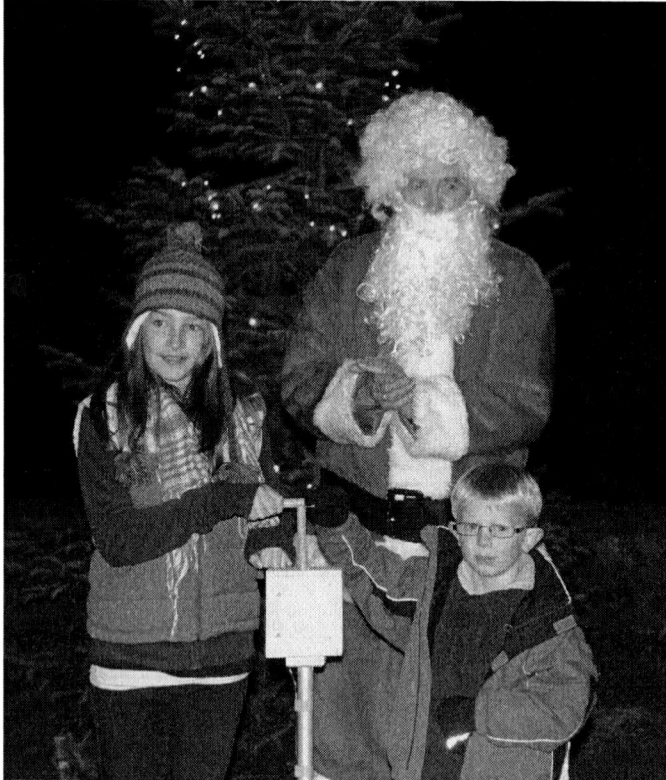

Lighting the Christmas Tree
Ella Gush and Nathaniel Bill, winners of the Christmas Colouring Competition help Santa Claus light the tree on 3rd December 2011.

Chapter 8 – VILLAGE SCHOOL
Langford Budville Church of England Primary School

The building was erected in 1851 for 80 children under the auspices of the Rev. T.H.Sotheby on part of his transferred glebe land. It was a National or Voluntary School for boys and girls, as well as a Sunday School which was held in the school room. It provided an elementary education funded by the National Society under the aegis of the Church of England.

In 1880 the Education Act required the attendance of all children at a school housed in a reasonable building with a qualified head teacher. Other Acts in the 1890s raised the school leaving age to 12 (in rural areas 11) and required education to be free. Private education had of course been available for those who could afford it and those institutions, now known as public schools, operated on a fee-paying basis as well as offering scholarships and bursaries. At the other end of the scale in some areas 'dame schools' were run in private houses, drawing pupils from the locality.

In 1896 the church was still educating 3 out of every 5 children and training two thirds of the teachers.

A 1902 Act created local Education Authorities and it was their duty to provide elementary, secondary and higher education in their areas and on 1st July 1903 Somerset County Council assumed responsibility for schools in our county. The Langford Budville School remains a voluntary controlled primary school under the auspices of the Church of England. In 1928 the government required enlargements at the school and £450 was raised – including the substantial sum of £250 from Colonel Leigh at Bindon.

It was noted on 2nd November 1900 that the School Managers asked the Chairman to inform the parents of Sam Stone, Thomas Brewer and Alf Williams that in future, damage done to the school property by their children would have to be made good by the parents, and that the managers should hold them responsible. Presumably as a result of this or similar behaviour, in 1901 the advisability of having a 'schoolmaster' was discussed and the outcome was that the then headteacher, Mrs. Sophia Palfrey, was asked to leave and was eventually replaced by a Mr. Hugh Davies.

If the children needed a tough approach, it appears that they got it with the arrival of Mr Davies, who was at the school from 1901 until 1935. Many stories prevail about how strict he was and how children were frightened of him. His temper was legendary. The School Managers' Minute Book shows their frustration at having to deal with this unacceptable behaviour towards both the children and themselves. In one instance he was asked to explain why he had been absent from class and on another occasion why he had sent the children home early. During the course of one of the interviews, Mr.Davies accused Mr. Albert Stone of being a 'liar'. An apology was a long time coming! One of the stories remembered is when he caned a boy so severely the cane broke and wedged in the blackboard! How times have changed. When Mr Davies died in 1945 it was recorded in the Wellington Weekly News *that he had been a well-known cricketer playing for Langford Budville and later a regular and valued member of the Wellington Home Team.* Perhaps he was good at whacking the ball!!

The registers show how adverse weather conditions, common childhood diseases and the necessity of helping in the home and fields – particularly at harvest time – played a part in absenteeism. School sometimes closed because of epidemics of such diseases as scarlet fever, whooping cough etc

Notes from the School log book:

1904 July 20th
Received this new log book today; also a thermometer

1904 Sept 30th
Today at the request of a parent, I gave a boy a caning for 'swearing and stealing apples from Albert Stone's (smithy) orchard'

1909 Nov 11th
Mrs. Davies away today from 11.00am – seeing 4 scholars to the oculist – were examined by Dr. Bendle and advised to wear glasses

1910 Jan 17th
School opened today with a poor attendance – the fumes given off by the paint after the stove was heated were so offensive we were obliged to remain outside for half an hour until all the paint was completely burnt away

1910 Sept 30th
Toothbrushes sold to children this week – 2d each

1911 March 28th
From a report by His Majesty's Inspector Mr. Tillard
'Reading and Recitation in the upper division are good on the whole but attention should be paid to clear enunciation, especially to the correct production of final consonants' (nothing changes!)
He continues *'There is little room for active exercises for the Babies Class.'*

1922 Dec 20th
School closes this afternoon for the Christmas vacation to reopen on Jan 8th 1923. Rev Swainson sent down a basketful of apples for the children; the teachers provided oranges.

In 1988 with only 22 pupils there was a concern that the school would close. However, under the determined leadership of Sylvia Gothard as chair of the action committee against the closure of the school, together with the chair of the school governors Mrs Susan Osborne, headmistress Mrs Wendy Nickels, parents and parishioners, the school was reprieved. Indeed it flourished and in the 1990s the then chair of governors, Mike Sertin tried to get a new and larger site, unfortunately without success.

Although currently there are only 7 children who reside in the parish and attend the school, it is nonetheless a marvellous asset to still have a village school after 161 years. Children currently come in by bus from Wellington to make up the requisite numbers. It is hoped that the school will long remain an integral part of the community.

Class of c1920/21
Alison Marguerite Salway (Margie) seated 2nd from left in the 2nd row with no-one in front of her.
Mr. H. Davies standing on the right – might the gentleman on the opposite end of the line be the Rev. Swainson?

Class of c1923
Back row: *Ernest Hayes, Fred Perry, Wilson Brewer, Thomas Perry, B.Hawkes, Ron Wood, George Maunder,*
Les Pike, Hector Wood, Aubrey Jones
Middle row: *Elsie Chipling, Hilda Chipling, Annie Waygood, Winnie Derbe, Mary Davis, Audrey Perry,*
Queenie Vickery, Violet Wood, Margaret Hawkes, Agnes Taylor, Edith Braddick,
Front row: *Ernest Pike, Albert Hayes, J. Fouracre, Reg Wood, Philip Salway, George Kidley*

Class of 1945 Big Room – Mrs Montague's class
Back row: *Lilian Broom, Mary Stevens, Bert Gamlin* 2nd row: *Brenda Wood, Joyce Brewer, Audrey Western, Doreen Jennings, Sheila Tooze, Mary Boone, Phyllis Townsend, Jim Jennings* 3rd row: *Gerald Brewer, Barbara Western, Donald Brewer, Dennis Stevens, Ann Toogood, Patricia Morgan*
Front row: *Tony Wood, Jack Jennings, David Percy*

Christmas in the Big Room c 1953
Santa Claus (maybe the Rev. W.L. Jones) hands a Xmas present to Valerie Brewer. Phyllis Jones is seated with Michael Jones on her knee. Very back row: *June Western, Eileen Western, Jennifer Perry*

Memories of a schoolboy – Alan Tucker

I can remember my first day at school in 1954 and how everything looked so big as we assembled in the 'lobby' at Langford School between the 'little room' where I was headed for the teaching of Mrs Brewer and the 'big room' where Miss Elwood would later preside. It was a two-room village school strong on the basics but I do not remember studying any science. As it was voluntary controlled the Vicar came in once a week and took a 'Bible' lesson. Swimming lessons were interesting because there was no water – chairs were taken out into the playground and the motions of breaststroke performed. Why we also played shinty, a hockey game with a bat and a ball, I will never know. Throwing rubber ringed quoits was more entertaining as we would mischievously throw one into the meadow behind the school.

Class of c1955 – Big Room – Miss Elwood
Left to right
Back row: *David Levett, Ann Levett, Martin Wotton, Marlene Basley, Roger Elliot, Eileen Western, Julian Fancy*
Middle row: *Gerald Gribble, Linda Hayman, Roger Wotton, Joy Jennings, Bill Townsend, Heather Gibbons, Christopher Shorney*
Front row: *Gilbert Gribble, John Howe, Sigrid Hanson, Geoffrey Saunders, Ruth Gibbons, Brian Smith, John Western, Andrew Ware*

Photo of makeshift swimming pool in the play ground in the 60's. Glyn Jones braving the water.

Photo of school taken from church Tower in 1967 and presented to Iris Brewer, teacher, on her retirement

School Staff c1986 – Left to right
Back row: *School assistant B. Pike, Rev. C. E. Rolfe, cook E. Drake, kitchen assistant D. Leighton*
Front row: *Caretaker B. Jones, teacher J. Hawkins, teacher Miss Dimbleby, ? ?, Lynn Rolfe*

Class of 1988 – Left to right
Back row: *Michael Glanfield, Daniel Dorrington, Peter Joslin, Robert Gothard.* 3rd row: *Sarah Cottrell, Caroline Howe, Andrew Gothard, Alexander Ash, Andrew Dorrington, Tammy Newstead, Amy Massey.*
2nd row: *? ? James Chilcott, Chris Massey, Raphael Phillips, ? ?*
Front row: *Matthew Barratt, Craig Fleming, Kathryn Harris, Annabelle Ash, Philippa Ash, Alex Goldsmith*

Class of 2012 – Left to right

Back Row: *Catherine Sharland (Higher Level Teaching Assistant), Chloe Towers, Harry West, George Barber, Tim Roberts, Alice Wilson-Hunt, Keith Sharpe (Head Teacher), Ella Crush, Robin McGuffie, Josie Kemble, Jasmine Newstead, Rita Derrick (Higher Level Teaching Assistant), Catherine Vincer (Senior Teacher)* Next Row: *Rebecca Dyer (Teaching Assistant), Karen Lockyer (Teaching Assistant), Russell Cheung, Jack Dyer, Oscar Kemble, Heidi Oaten, Isobel Finucane-Fenn, Olivia Hunter, Olivia Jones.* Next Row: *Alix Redwood Joseph Burton, Xander Bogan-Chandler, Dillon Batstone, Morgan Smith, Ellie-Mae Towers, Nathanael Ray.* Next Row: *Charlie Ray, Jae Veysey-Milton, Tilly Rowse, Amber Finucane-Fenn, Katiann Perry, Jack Dennett, Keely Batstone, Zac Bogan-Chandler, Aiden Short.* Next Row: *Mischa Veysey-Millen, Ruby Marlow, Amy Baxter, Matthew Humble, Harry Jenkins, Jacob Norman, Layla Batstone.* Front Row kneeling: *Faith Smith, Breeanne Batstone, Lily Dyer, Charlie Cable, Joseph Bond, Charlie Norman, Oliver Dennett, Adam Johnson, Jamie Towers*

Retirement of Judi Tregillus, & Joy Eady who had the 'joy' of living in the village & walking each day to school where she taught from 1988 – 2010

Head teachers at the school since its inception. Many from later years are remembered fondly. Sourced from Kelly's directory (K) and Binns's Register (B) which do not always tally.

1861	Miss Caroline Elizabeth Jenkins (K)	
1866	Ditto	
1872	Miss Priscilla Griffiths (K)	
1875	Ditto	
1878 - Feb	L.E.D.Turner (B)	Took charge
1881 - Feb	Master - Lister Clegg (B)	In census he is 21 yrs old & living in school house. Betsy Blackmore aged 47 is school mistress living with a widowed mother of 78 in one of 6 dwellings called Bowerings Place or Cottages.
1883	Master - Lister Clegg (K)	
1883	H. Stubbs (B)	Left 3rd Aug 1888 Also an instructor of the church band & secretary of The Working Men's Club
10th Sept 1888	Master - F. W. Mathews (B)	Left 5th Aug 1893
1889	Master - Frederick Mathews (K)	Av. Attendance 53
1894	Ditto (K)	
20th Sept 1893	Sophia Palfrey (B)	
1897	Mrs Sophia Palfrey (K)	Left 31st Oct 1901 Miss C. Dowling infants
1902	Ditto (K)	Mrs H. Davies infants 1st Feb 1900 Mrs. H. Davies recognised as an uncertified teacher at a salary of £4 p.a.
3rd Nov 1901	Hugh Davies M.R.S.T. (B)	
1906	Hugh Davies (K)	
1910	Ditto	
1914	Ditto	
1919	Ditto	
1923	Ditto	
1907	Ditto	
1931	Ditto	
1935 31st May	Ditto	
1st July 1935	Dorothy Montague (B)	Left 12th March 1949
14th March 1949	Miss Kathleen M. Elwood (B)	Left 17th March 1967 as did Mrs. I. Brewer asst. teacher for over 30 years
??????	*Have been unable to ascertain*	
In 1980s	Mrs Wendy Nickels	Left July 1991
Sept 1991	Mrs Wendy Pollard	Left Aug 1997
Sept 1997-2001	Mrs Irene Maddocks	Left Dec 2001
Jan 2001	Acting Head Deborah Bishop	Left Dec 2002
Jan-Sept 2002	Temporary Head Keith Sharpe	
2002	Catherine Groves	
2005	Keith Sharpe	

Chapter 9 – FROM A WORKING MEN'S CLUB TO A VILLAGE HALL 1856 - 2012

As early as the 1840s the resident curate – M. Campbell – was considering the merits of founding a Working Men's Club. It was thought to be beneficial to provide a facility where working men and lads (not less than 16 years of age) could meet and relax together – other than the pub! In 1856 the Reverend T.H. Sotheby (then Vicar of Milverton) founded the first Working Men's Club in Langford Budville. It first met in the school and then subsequently in 2 rooms in one of his cottages as both a Working Men's Club and a Reading Room. It is thought that the cottage in question is now called Teazel Cottage as the current owners – the Bills – recently discovered indications of a skittle alley on the top floor. It is recorded that, a few years later, Mr. C. Lamport of Bindon House in the 1880s became one of the organisers of the Club, with Mr. Stubbs, schoolmaster, as secretary. William Brewer was caretaker in 1883 and Fred Hancock in1889.

As time went by it was felt that an effort should be made to obtain larger and more suitable accommodation than the 2 comparatively small rooms. So in 1900 E.C.A Sanford Esq., agreed to the purchase of some land owned by Mr. J.E. Gamlin for the sole purpose of building a Working Men's Club (where Tree Tops is now situated in Butts Lane). This he duly did and, after plans and specifications drawn were up by Mr. W. Gilbert Comley (clerk of works to Nynyehead Estates) and money was raised from an appeal, the hall was finally built and vested in the hands of 4 Trustees, namely E.C.A Sanford (Nynehead Court), T.H.T. Winwood (Wellisford Manor), Albert Stone (blacksmith) and the Reverend C.H. Luxton. The building was constructed of corrugated iron and consisted of a hall (40' by 20') with 2 ante-rooms and a skittle alley adjoining.

Chy-an-mor to Butts Cottages – left to right – with Village Hall centre on a fine washing day

Working Men's Club c1940
A special gathering (but no one knows what for)
A number of faces have been indentified but memory may have caused the odd discrepancy. Appearing
in this photo are: Eunice Hayes, Clara Scribbens, Geoffrey Braddick, Rodney Jones, Cissie Hayes,
Wilfred Coles, Albert Hayes, Walter Harris – ready with his violin for the entertainment, Reg Locke,
Flora Harris, Phyllis Jones, Nancy (Annie) Jones, Minnie Jones, Mrs Hayes, Mrs Braddick, Eva
Burgess, Reg Stone, Doris Stone, Elsie Brewer, Wilson Brewer, Irene Greedy, Mrs Scribbens, Hilda
Harris, Jack Harris, Sidney Derbe, Grace Hayes, Joe Hayes

It was recorded in the *Wellington Weekly News* that the club was opened on 12th January 1910 by Colonel Sanford, in the presence of Mr. Carlton Cross, Mr. John Winwood (who represented his father Mr. T.H.R Winwood – president of the Club), Mr.Parnell, the Honourable Secretary and Treasurer the Reverend C.H. Luxton. In the afternoon 18 children were entertained to tea and games made possible by money raised by the 'Christmas Waits' (carol singing) and in the evening the doors were thrown open to 140 parishioners from 7.30-12.30pm. In April that year the WWN notes that a team of single men beat the married men by 39 pins in a skittle match to mark the opening of the new skittle alley.

From 1902 Kelly's directory notes Jonathan Perry is in place as caretaker followed by Mrs H. Harris in 1927. Discovered in the archives were Rules for a Langford Budville Workmen's Club Outing League for which they paid weekly subscriptions and if they paid 5 shillings per annum they became Honorary Members of the League. One can only assume that they had many exciting annual outings. Sadly there are no records of where they went.

Through the decades the clubhouse was used for a variety of village functions – skittles, darts, dances, meetings, parties etc. and especially when the community needed to get together to celebrate. There are many references to events mentioned in the *Wellington Weekly News* – notably the end of the 1st & 2nd World Wars and Royal celebrations.

In the *Wellington Weekly News* on 13th June 1945 an article about the Welcome Home fund activities states that *it was resolved that all monies raised in excess of £250 be allocated to a fund for the improvement of the social amenities of the village. Although the precise nature of these are not to be agreed yet, it was evident that the meeting was fully alive to the need for a properly equipped Village Community Centre.*

During the 2nd world war the two rooms were used as classrooms for evacuees – about 14 in number – and the school paid rent; a revenue of £70.80 was noted. During the 1950s activities continued but membership dwindled. In the initial covenant it had been stated that if the membership fell below 12, ownership of the club would revert to the trustees and/or their beneficiaries. Membership had in fact fallen below the statutory number of 12 during 1941/2 and as such the Club had therefore been running illegally although Mr. W. Sanford, the benficial owner was unaware of this situation. Mr. Thomas Fox – Treasurer of the Club notes, in a declaration dated 1979, that the Club had ceased to function in 1956.

On 12th April 1967 a public meeting was called to discuss what steps could be taken to have the building transferred to the village for use as a village hall, but with no tangible outcome and, in 1981, after legal negotiations the hall was sold and subsequently knocked down.

In February 1981 the Reverend C.E. Rolfe wrote in the Parish Magazine:

'A New Village Hall' – how exciting is it to hear of the plans to build a hall in the village. There is no doubt about the need for such a building. There is a strong community spirit present in Langford Budville and a public building of this sort will be a tremendous help in fostering it. St. Peter's Church will do all it can in supporting this venture'

1977-2003 Gerald & Ann Brewer remember:

'One Spring evening in 1977 a Public Meeting was called in the school, asking people for suggestions for the celebration of H.M. Queen Elizabeth's Silver Jubilee – time was swiftly running out as the big day was 2nd June. The upshot of this meeting was Gerald Brewer agreeing to gather a group of people together to organise a Fete and Tea Party plus Children's Fancy Dress competition for the afternoon, followed by Mr. R. Keyworth and the (then prominent) Project Committee arranging a BBQ. All the events were held in the grounds of The Martlet by kind permission of Gwyn and Pete Harris – mine hosts at that time.

All above events were a resounding success with the upshot being that the Fete raised well over £100 (a princely sum at that time) which then begged the question – how could this sum best be spent to benefit the parishioners. Eventually an over 60's Christmas Dinner and Party was arranged. This event proved to be so popular that it was to continue until the school lost its cooking facilities. During these years a group of people met every Monday evening from 2nd week in September up until the party date in February by kind invitation of Robert and Ann Vellacott to plan details of meals and to rehearse the entertainment. And so – one evening it was mooted that we were desperately in need of a Village Hall, so that not only this event, but so many others would be catered for. This would save the hassle of having to traverse the area collecting tables etc and clearing the school premises quickly. At this time there was nowhere to hold an event in the village – The Working Men's Club having been long defunct and in a state of ruin.

Pram Race August 1977 Gerald as mum and Ann as baby.

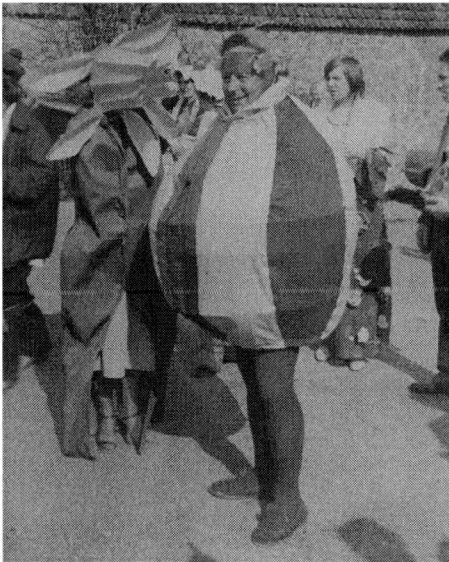

Easter Parade 1977 Gerald as an egg and Ann as a daffodil.

Hence it was agreed from then on that we would do our utmost to put a plan into action – to obtain a Village Hall.

A meeting was called in the Church in May 1983 and whilst some opposition was voiced it was voted to go ahead and a committee was elected.

The first site made available was Three Ashes (later to be found unsuitable for use by the school) thereby giving us a chance to commence fundraising with many varied events including an Annual Fete, Vintage Rally – Pram Races (themed), Fireworks & Bonfire, Easter Bonnet Parade, Outdoor Skittle Week, Dinner Dances, BBQ's, Horse Race Nights – 200 Club(£600 draw at Christmas). There was also a fortnightly Bingo Session at Milverton. Other activities were held outside the village, although at times this was to prove a somewhat arduous task, very few fell by the wayside such was the enthusiasm shown.

A parish survey was delivered to every household in the Parish enabling everyone to vote and state points of view. These were counted one Saturday evening in the church by an independent band of people. However our own recording officer for the evening – the late Mr. Norman Ware – expressed his pleasure in announcing a result of 4-1 in favour of continuing with the project.

So fund raising continued which received a boost in 1987 from the closure of the Village Chapel - £35,265 - for which everyone was exceedingly grateful.

Then there came a bitter blow to our aspirations. In 1999 we were very close to obtaining a site at Petersmead behind the school. Unfortunately this did not materialise as a group of local residents in close proximity to the site purchased the land.

After this, with no site in view nor at that time did there seem to be any prospect of one, we had a very quiet few years. During this time we lost many prolific fund raisers. Some left the area for pastures new, and others, sadly, are no longer with us: to name just 5 of our hardest workers John Sweet, Frank Gage, Bill Brooks, and Ann & Robert Vellacott. There were many more, too many to list here and to whom we remain grateful.

In 2003 Gerald Brewer handed over the chair of the Village Hall Steering Committee and thankfully now we are in 2012 and within the sight of the much and long-awaited hall.

The Final Phase – Some Facts and Figures

2002

Risons (Ritherdons) Lane site made available by Cottrell family (It had been long-listed in 1997 but rejected in favour of Petersmead). Peter Barnes commissioned to produce a hall design based on the plans in existence for the Petersmead site. The hall specifications were based on the outcome of the village survey conducted in 1997 and were available early in 2003.

2003

Ashley Vellacott became Chairman. Committee resolved to submit planning application for the Ritherdons Lane site and to investigate sources of funding in addition to funds already held in trust. Considered an alternative site East of the church (which had also been on the 1997 long list) and favoured by a considerable number of villagers, but following advice from the Chief Planning Officer the site was rejected on several grounds.

2004

Planning applications submitted, and resubmitted, leading to planning consent granted on the Ritherdons Lane site with a total of 19 conditions which included improvements to the lane and junction to meet Highway Dept's reservations.

2005

October – New Village Hall Management Committee formed after public meeting in the school – Mike Sertin persuaded Keith Moore to become Chairman.
November – Committee members became Trustees of the Village Hall registered charity.
December – Village Hall Survey sent to all families seeking views on the hall project. The findings subsequently demonstrated to the Big Lottery that there was a genuine need for the community building.

2006

March – Village Hall logo designed by pupils of Langford Budville School.

April – October Draft business plan produced and applications for grants made to TDBC, SCC and Big Lottery Community Buildings Fund.

2007

Grants agreed by County, District and Parish Councils. Fund raising concert featuring the Wurzels in Bere Barn.

2008

March – Negotiations began with Somerset Wildlife Trust over the acquisition of land at Two Ash Triangle for road improvements.

September – Big Lottery Fund awarded the project almost £400,000. One of only nine awards in the South West.

October – Natural England confirmed that the project would have no detrimental effect on the SSSI status of the Langford Heathfield Nature Reserve.

November – Wildlife survey by independent consultants confirmed no issues with protected species.

December – Peter Barnes as Project Manager and John Hannon as Construction Design and Management Co-ordinator were appointed.

2009

April – Big Lottery Fund extended period of grant to October 2009 to allow for delays caused in connection with land acquisition.

August – Agreement in principle with SWT to purchase land for road improvements.

September – Big Lottery agreed to 2nd extension to March 2010.

November – Main contractors appointed.

December – TDBC grant planning consent extension adding a condition for a further wildlife survey.

2010

February – Big Lottery Fund agreed to third time extension to May 2010.

March – Second wildlife survey completed by independent consultants again reveals no issues with wildlife. Application made to Planning Inspectorate to de-register as common land areas acquired from SWT.

April - Big Lottery Fund awarded a top up grant of £98,395 and agreed to a 4th extension to September 2010.

June – All land transfers completed and deeds of title lodged with land registry.

August – Site inspection by Planning Inspectorate re de-registration of Common Land.

September – Big Lottery agreed further extension to time period for grant.

October – Planning Inspectorate agreed de-registration of Common Land (7 months after application).

2011

February – Enabling works commenced consisting of translocation of hedge bank under supervision of wildlife consultant.

March – Applications for utility connections.
April – Sub-committees commenced work on hire charge schemes, licensing agreements and website design.
June – Application made to TDBC to discharge all remaining planning conditions.
Nov – Contract signed with main contractor.
December – Ground works contractor commenced.

2012
January – Discussions and agreement with main contractors on final design details for hall building.
February – Road and drainage work completed. Lane re-opened to traffic – Village school commenced work on time capsule to be installed under the hall.
March – Preparation of hall site and foundations laid.

Village Hall under construction in May 2012

Chapter 10 – **SPORT & LEISURE**

In earlier times leisure time was scarce for ordinary folk as they spent most of their time earning a living just to survive. People's lives would have revolved mainly round church activities and the village itself and they had to rely on making their own entertainment. They would have looked forward to church festivals and seasonal celebrations – Christmas, Easter, Saints Days and the Harvest. The famous one connected with the village was known as the Langford Revels which took place during the week of the Feast of Saints Peter and Paul, June 29th.

This event provided the Church with an important source of income through the sale of copious quantities of Church Ale which, at least until the mid-17th century, was apparently dispensed from Church House, beside the Church itself. A ceremony was involved called 'clipping the tower'. In it, the villagers formed a ring around the Church and circled it until two leaders broke ranks and went to the Church walls. At that point the entire company approached the Church, giving out three almighty shouts with the objective of frightening away the Devil. The bells were then rung to hasten the Devil on his way and it has been suggested that he was encouraged to head for Thorne St Margaret. Of course, on St Margaret's Day the people of Thorne St Margaret would ring their bells to chase him back again.

During the Puritan interregnum of 1649 – 1660, the authorities sought to suppress the event:

> In 1649 the JPs for Somerset re-issued the old orders against village revels. In 1650 they were defied at Langford Budville in the Vale of Taunton Deane, there was 'fiddling and dancing and a great rout of people'. A tithing man bringing the justices' ruling was chased away by a group of Wellington men shouting 'We will keep revel in despite of all such tithing calves as thou art'.

Revels of this sort were common in the West Country and were often called 'Church Ales'; they allowed the working people to let off steam and the churches to raise funds, but not infrequently descended into drunkenness, violence and debauchery.

A more blatantly reckless pastime called 'cudgel-playing' is said to have been popular in Langford Budville and Holywell Lake. A raised platform was erected before a public house or in any open space, by setting a pair of barrels upright on the ground and placing planks across the top. One man jumped onto the platform, stripped off his shirt and flourished a stick. Another would take up the challenge and climb up onto the boards with his own cudgel and they would then set about each other until one was forced off the platform. Both were usually badly wounded.

Cider wassailing was and still is a tradition taking place in apple orchards on 17th January, which is the old Julian Calendar's 12th Night, when people gather to chase away any evil spirits which might harm the harvest – firing shotguns and banging drums as well as drinking lots of cider.

Inns were of course convivial meeting places, but these were mainly for the men folk. For much of the 19th century three inns are mentioned in the Langford Budville censuses – The Hare & Hounds at Bindon, The Crown (now the Martlet) and The New Inn, which was in Old Post.

The Church had a band which played in the gallery to accompany the hymns before an organ was installed in 1838. Choir and bell ringing practice would also have provided recreation for a few after the drudgery of work. Bell ringing in years gone by was often a secular activity used on royal occasions or peace celebrations and even as a summons to people to work in the fields. By the 19th century it became more closely associated with Church events.

Rugby

The latter part of the 19th century saw an increase in sporting activities in the area as indicated by the photograph showing that Langford Budville had its very own rugby team which probably continued through until the outbreak of the 1st World War.

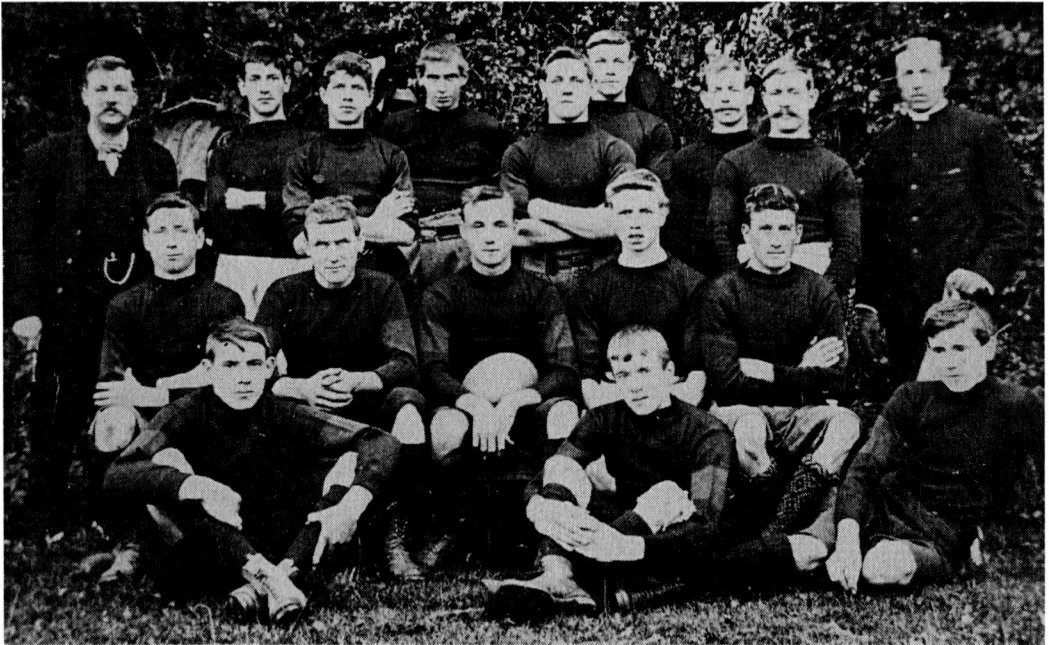

Langford Budville Rugby Football team 1897-8 Season
Back row: *2ⁿᵈ player from the left Walter Perry* – Left gentleman: *William Victor Braddick*
Right gentleman: *Reverend C.H. Luxton* – Centre with the ball *William Stephen Braddick*

Wellington Weekly reports – 13th October 1897
Langford Budville v. Rowbarton
These teams met at Langford Budville on Saturday last. Langford is a newly formed Club, and this being their first match, much interest was manifested in the game, which brought a good gate. The home team lined out as follows: Back, W. Perry; threequarters, W. Braddick (Capt), Jennings, Vickery and Rossiter; halves, Jenkins and R. Perry; forwards, Burston, Pike, Palmer, Paul, Burgess, Kidley, Hurley and F. Braddick. The visitors had their full strength, and played well, but the home team had the best of the game throughout and won by 2 goals 4 tries (22 points) to a try. The try getters for Langford were Jennings (2), Vickery, Burston, W. Braddick and F. Braddick. W. Braddick kicked the goals.

As yet no one has been able to say where they played – maybe on the the field at the top of Ritherdons Lane across the road from the new village hall?

Walter Perry

Cricket

Nynehead & Langford Budville Cricket Club 1902
Second from left back row – *William Stephen Braddick*
Centre with the bat – *Reverend C.H. Luxton*

Cricket

In 1901 Langford Budville joined forces with Nynehead to form a cricket team, with the Reverend C.H. Luxton, Vicar of Langford Budville, as captain. The President was W.A.Sanford, Vice-Presidents Col. E.C.A. Sanford, C. Pole-Carew, T.H.R. Winwood, H. Worthington, J. Kinder and H. Ewens; Secretary and Treasurer Rev. H.C. Launder (Vicar of Nynehead); Vice-Captain H. Merry; committee S. Kidley, W. Comley, F. Jenkins, A. Taylor and W. Pike. The cricket pitch was situated on a field to the north-west of Nynehead Court.

We are unsure how long the cricket connection with Nynehead lasted but we have noted that in later years a number of our players went to play for the Wellington Home Team.

Langford Heathfield Golf Club

Work commenced on the 9-hole golf course on the Common in Langford Budville on 3rd March 1908 and it was opened by Col. E.C. Sanford on 7th July 1909. It was finally wound up on 31st October 1925.

On March 9th 1911 the Wellington Weekly News carried a report on the Langford Heathfield Golf Club AGM. Less than two years since it opened, the Club had a membership of 101. Members were told that the drainage work which had been undertaken had stood up well to the record rainfall! The joining fee was £1/1s/0d and the annual subscription was the same amount – sums that will make today's golfers green with envy.

The course was open six days a week, being closed on Sundays. The first hole was 365 yards and was of the dog-leg variety. James Hayes was the first green keeper and Frederick Jones a later one.

People today remember their fathers saying that as boys they would go and look for golf balls as a way of earning some pocket money. Remains of some of the bunkers can still be seen on the Heath.

The clubhouse was not actually on the main part of the common where the course was situated but stood on the opposite side of the road, near Middle Hill Farm. It seems that after the closure of the course the Broom family of Middle Hill Farm sold the clubhouse to a Mr Milnes Priscott of Milverton, who used to run Nunnington Park Farm. The clubhouse was moved to Nunnington Park and Glyn Jones discovered it in 2011 still in the grounds of the farm

Sue Cottrell of Bere Farm still has an interesting piece of golfing memorabilia – a silver snuff box presented to her grandfather, E.W. Ebdon Esq, by members of the Langford Heathfield Golf Club in 1919.

Skittles

The game of skittles has been a West Country sport for decades usually played in leagues in pub-alleys, although the former Langford Budville Working Men's Club did have its own designated alley. Sadly, The Martlet Inn lost its alley in 2007 for use as a function room.

The clubhouse today

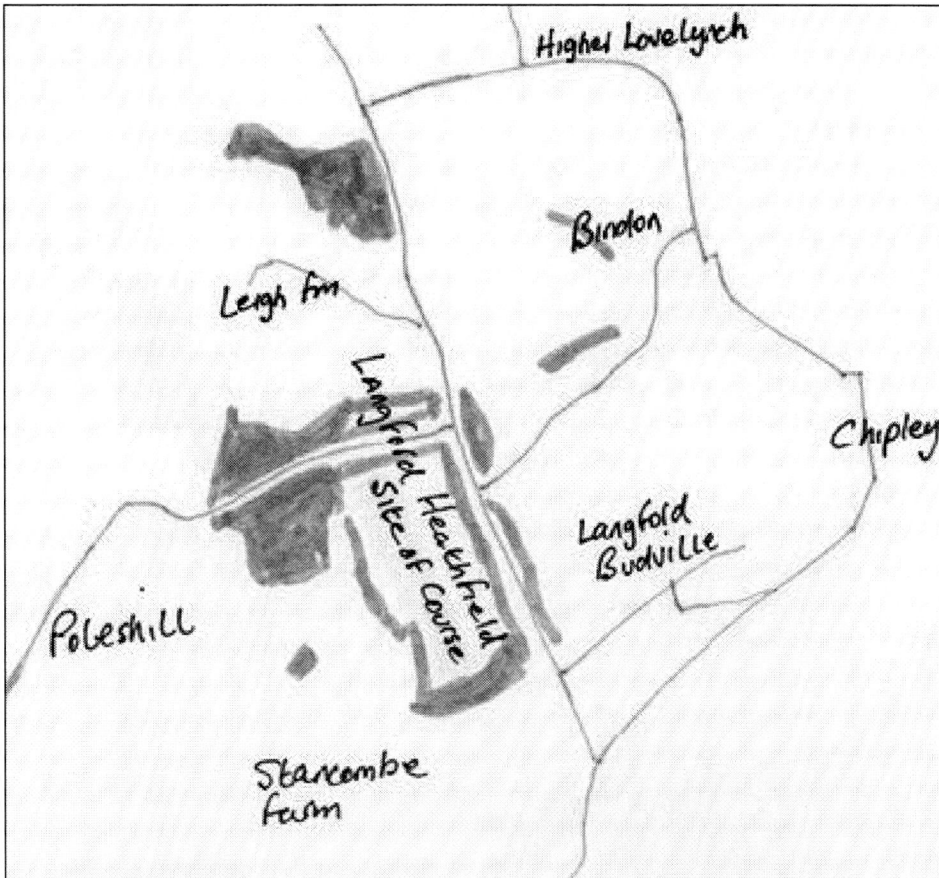

A sketch map of the location of the golf course

The Annual Children's Sports

The Annual Children's Sports were held in August and in 1920 the Wellington Weekly News records:

> *From the proceeds of a successful skittle tournament held earlier in the year at the Working Men's club, the Sports Committee were again enabled to organise children's sports, held in Oddmeads field kindly lent by Mr. G. Parnell…the Wellington Town Band enlivened the proceedings and a sumptuous tea was served in the Working Men's Club.*
>
> *When all the races had been run – potato sack, three-legged, egg and spoon, skipping, boot and coat, threading needle, backward running, long jump, high jump, flat, throwing cricket ball/tennis ball, quarter-mile, consolation and bandsmen's race – and prizes awarded, dancing took place for the remainder of the time on Colonel and Mrs. Howard's lawn of Oddmeads House.*

All sounds great fun although today a number of the afore-mentioned races would not be allowed under current health and safety rules!

Footpaths & Bridleways

In olden times if you hadn't got a horse you walked everywhere. Now we choose to ride or walk often as a leisure pastime. We are very lucky that Langford Budville is criss-crossed with a number of footpaths and bridleways to tempt us to explore the beautiful surrounding countryside. We are grateful to Zenah Rowe, our current Parish Footpaths Officer, who ensures that the paths are easily accessible and stiles kept in good condition. For the past few years during the summer months she has organised early evening guided walks for us to enjoy, starting usually at Langford Heathfield Common.

Langford Heathfield Nature Reserve

The village is fortunate to have an extensive nature reserve on its doorstep, open to public access and much used by local people for recreation. Langford Heathfield lies alongside the Langford Budville to Wiveliscombe road and comprises 226 acres of woodland, heathland and scrub; it also includes some small ponds and brooks. The area is owned and managed by the Somerset Wildlife Trust and is their second largest site. The Trust purchased the main site from the Sanford estate in 1982 and added Coram's Wood, in the north-west sector towards Poleshill, and Lucas's Copse on the west side towards Stancombe, in 1985. Langford Heathfield is a Site of Special Scientific Interest (SSSI).

Between 1909 and 1925, an area in the north of the reserve was used for a 9-hole golf course, but there is little trace of this remaining today. At the far southern end is a small area called The Dips, incorporating an old quarry, where children have a bike track. However, the chief recreational use of the reserve is for walking, and there are numerous tracks threading through the woods and across the clearings. In the wetter areas, the Trust maintains raised duck-walks to traverse the mud.

Much of the reserve is common land, known in the 16th century by the alternative name of Whitmore, and some local properties still retain ancient rights of pasturage (grazing), turbary (turf cutting) and estovers (woodcutting for fencing and firewood). Ponies still graze open parts of the heath and help to keep the invading scrub and coarse grasses under control. Due to its status as common land and to the predominantly damp conditions, the land has not been reclaimed or improved for agriculture, thus enabling the survival of an extensive and varied flora and fauna.

Areas of ancient woodland consist mainly of ash and field maple, which are not averse to damp soil, with frequent oak and beech standards. In the even wetter places near the streams, alder stands occur, and in the secondary woodland (ie more recent growth on what may previously have been grazing land) birch, ash and willow predominate around some larger oaks. The understorey is dominated by hazel and bramble, but field maple, holly and hawthorn are also plentiful, together with spindle and woody nightshade.

In 1906 Col and Mrs Sanford planted a walnut tree on the Common, almost opposite where Hilltop now stands, to commemorate the birth of their son William Charles Ayshford Sanford. A ceremony was held together with an address by the vicar and a brass plate and railings were put in place. The railings and name plate have long gone but the tree still stands.

The many wildflower species reflect the varied soil conditions of the dry heathland, damp fen grassland and woodland. Two species of orchid grow in Langford Heathfield and some relatively scarce species may be found, such as bog pimpernel and pale dog-violet. There are several recorded species of fern (including the ubiquitous bracken) and lichen, and fungi are abundant.

In addition to common mammals such as the not entirely welcome grey squirrel and badger, the site contains colonies of dormice, and roe deer are occasionally seen. Pipistrelle, serotine and the rare lesser horseshoe bat have all been recorded, while the ponds and wet areas are home to frogs, toads and newts. Adders and common lizards can be seen in the dryer grassland.

A diverse range of bird species has been recorded. In addition to the commoner species that one may encounter locally elsewhere, tree pipit, lesser spotted woodpecker, redstart and pied flycatcher have all bred in the reserve. In the past, Langford Heathfield was a breeding territory for nightingale and grasshopper warbler – how good it would be to hear those calls once again!

Around 30 species of butterfly have been recorded, which amounts to nearly half the entire British list. Notable among this impressive total are the sadly declining Small Pearl-bordered Fritillary and the Brown Hairstreak. The Somerset Moth Group occasionally traps (and releases) on the reserve and some nationally scarce moth species have been recorded.

Women's Institute

The Women's Institute Movement in Britain started in 1915, during First World War, to encourage countrywomen to get involved in the growing and preserving of food to help increase the supply of food to the 'war-torn' nation. It was a huge success and by the end of the war in 1918 there were 199 W.I.s and 37 county federations; by 1919 the total number of W.I.s had reached 1,405.

Langford Budville W.I. followed on closely and formed in 1920. At the Somerset Heritage Centre there are detailed accounts of the meetings held throughout its active years, indicating a membership of between 45-50 until it closed in 1944, by which time numbers had fallen back to 19.

The Wellington Weekly News often highlighted W.I. events:

20th January 1937 –Mrs. Forster of Wellisford Manor presided. A demonstration on 'Anti Gas Attacks' was given by Capt. Gage-Browne, who impressed upon the members that 'Prevention is better than cure', this being the motto for the month. Afterwards gas masks* were handed round and tried on. After tea community singing was much enjoyed. A competition for 'something new from something old' was won by Miss Toogood from Beer Farm, who made a marvellous rug out of bits of wool. It was unanimously decided that Mrs. Bennallacks' services as trainer of the drama members should be acknowledged with a gift. The members performed their play on 11th January when they visited Sampford Peverell. The afternoon closed with the National Anthem.'

*38 million masks were issued in Britain at the start of the war, but thankfully these were never needed.

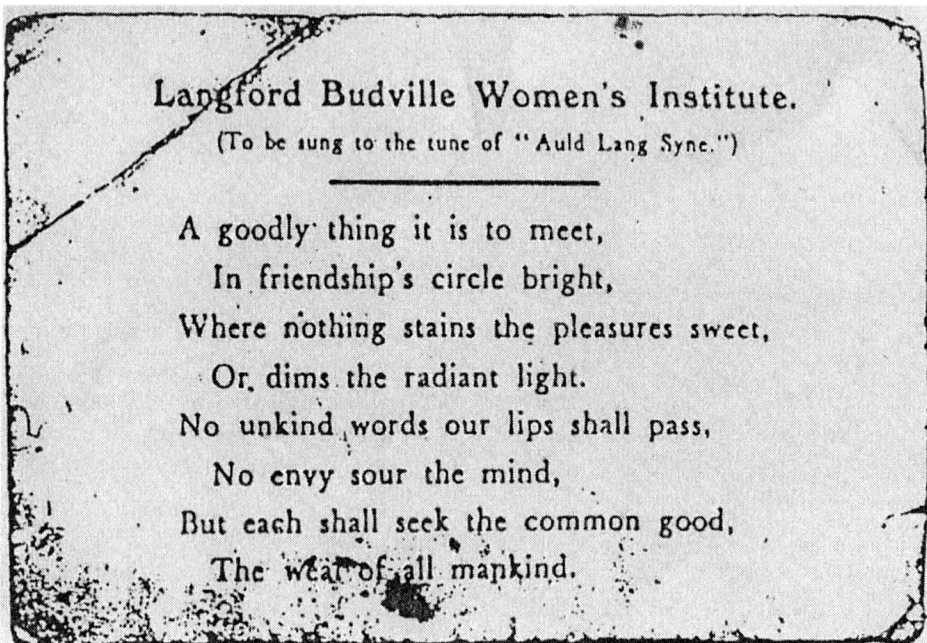

Langford Budville Women's Institute Song

Langford Ladies

Margaret Brown records:

The inaugural committee meeting of the Langford Budville Ladies Social Club took place at the Vicarage on Wednesday 18th November 1964 at 11.00 am. It was envisaged that eventually they might re-form the W.I. but a larger number of members was required.

Present were Mrs Scott, Mrs Fox, Mrs Ware, Mrs Case and Mrs Evans. It was agreed to hold meetings on the second Friday of each month at 7.30 pm with a subscription of 6 shillings per annum. Mrs Fox agreed to hold the first meeting in her house, Croxhall, on 10th December and to find a speaker. There would be a charge of 6 pence for refreshments. A draw (raffle) and a competition would be held at each meeting. A year later it was decided to fine members one penny if they didn't enter the competition!

The First Committee comprised:

	President	Mrs Fox
	Secretary	Mrs West
	Treasurer	Mrs Siderfin
	Mrs Scott	Mrs Braddick

The early meetings included talks on: Fire prevention in the home, Demonstration of Dorset embroidery, beekeeping, a visit to Holland by members, sewing machines, first aid.

It was not easy to arrange visits in those days as fewer members had cars. Coaches were booked for special outings to the theatre in Bristol and the coast in the summer.

In April 1965 a vote was taken as to whether the club wanted to become a W.I. but the proposal was rejected. During the 1960s the numbers grew with members joining from the surrounding area and there were 29 paid up members in 1970. As the numbers grew, meetings transferred to the School.

In the 1980s Nora Smith became an important member of the club taking over as President and keeping the minutes. She held on to all the early records and kept a register of members for the rest of her life. Many fondly remember her cheese biscuits, which she unfailingly produced at meetings, and also recall that she was game to have a go at anything. She must have been well into her 80s when the Ladies took her Ten Pin Bowling for the first time.

During the early 1990s the numbers began to fall and several members left to join the local Women's Institute at Appley Cross, whose events are regularly featured in the Langford Budville parish magazine. It was then decided to meet in members' houses to keep down the cost, rather than rent the schoolroom.

Photo from Wellington Weekly News *November 1990*
25th Anniversary - celebration dinner at the Beam Bridge Hotel Wellington
Mrs. O Scott and Mrs A Fox were founder members along with Mrs Freda Evans and Mrs A. Case.
Back row: *Janet Beazley, Joan Tytler, Sylvia Gothard, Anne Harris, Ann Hendy, Lesley Blackmore, Madeleine Anderson, Joy Yendall, Maureen Batstone, Maggie Ashmore*
Middle row: *Unknown, Nora Smith, Joan Pearse, Mrs Wyatt*
Seated: *Maureen Thompson, Ann Case, Alix Fox, Freda Evans, Midge Matthews, Mary Woodley*

Langford Ladies Now

Nowadays we are far less formal. We gave up having a committee and a chairman several years ago and decide on our programme for the year at our Christmas meal in January. Members come up with ideas and organise them on a monthly rota.

We have a current membership of twenty and meet in each others houses or go on organised visits. Hopefully we will soon have the use of our new village hall for meetings when necessary. Our meetings recently have included a murder mystery walk around Wellington, a visit to Nynehead Court Gardens, theatre trips, book reviews and discussions.

Photo August 2011 at the Gothards, South Gundenham – Annual Summer Barbecue
Back row: *Julie Carter, Sylvia Gothard*
Middle row standing: *Wendy Thomas, Alison Toogood, Jeannette Hare, Laurian Cooper, Marjorie Stockley, Sarah Nutt, Jean Marshall*
Seated: *Margaret Brown, Anne Harris, Lynne Moore.*
[Anne Harris & Sylvia Gothard are in both photos]

The Village Fete

The Village Fete has taken on various guises over the years and taken place in a variety of locations in the village, usually in the summer. However, it has always been an opportunity for village folk to gather together and enjoy some fun as well as spend a little money. The Church in recent years took on the onus of organising the Fete but last year a designated Village Fete committee was formed, comprising representatives from various village organisations. Their first Fete, held in July 2011 on the Triangle, was a huge success. It included a classic car display, a dog show, side shows, circus skills, village history exhibition, cream teas, BBQ, bric-a–brac, a wood turner etc. It is hoped that this year's Fete, to be held on 14th July, will be another enjoyable occasion when it features the Wellington Majorettes as the opening event.

Music & Mirth

Home-grown entertainment has always been part of village. Our earliest photo is of young folk dressed in a variety of costume in 1905 in the grounds of Springwood – we can only conjecture what the occasion is.

Young entertainers, Springwood 1905

Dances were held regularly on Saturday evenings for many years in the Working Men's Club with the music being played by local musicians – well-remembered names are Walter Harris on violin and Ann Vellacott on the piano.

During the 1970s/80s, pensioners were entertained annually in the school hall, enjoying a supper followed by the Langford Entertainers – some names to recall who tripped the light fantastic: Gerald and Ann Brewer, Ann and Robert Vellacott, Sandra and Frank Gage, The Kavanagh family

History repeating itself – Sally Pritchard repeated this performance, in fish-net tights in *Village Varieties – an Old Time Music Hall* in the Function Room at the Martlet Inn in 2009 – but sadly there is no photograph.

Ann Vellacott – singing Burlington Bertie at the Pensioner's Party c1980

Pensioner's Party c1979 A good time had by all
Left to right back row: *Mr Robert Vellacott, Mr Gerald Brewer, Mrs Ann Vellacott, Mr John Sweet,*
Mr Peter Harris (Martlet landlord), Mr Paul Rockett (policeman)
Next row: *Mr Taylor, Mr Cushion, Mrs Cushion, Mrs Vellacott, Mr W. Harris, Mrs W. Batstone,*
Mrs Joan Wotton, Mr Jack Wotton, Mrs E. Thatcher
Next row: *Mr Holway, Mrs Holway, Mrs White, Mr White, Mrs Braddick, Mrs H. Harris,*
Mrs L. Pike, Mr Les Pike
Next row: *Mrs Dorothy Western, Mr Jack Western, Mr Rodney Jones, Mrs Phyllis Jones,*
Mr Aubrey Jones, Mrs Betty Jones, Mrs Evans.
At the front: *Mrs Elsie Brewer, Mrs Mary Brewer, Mr Wilson Brewer*

In the past few years, under the direction of Duncan Hughes and Marjorie Stockley, there have been a number of shows performed in the function room of The Martlet in aid of charity – namely Village Varieties, A Miscellany of Music & Mirth, Sing Along With Us and Under Milk Wood (also performed in the Church). Money raised for St. Margaret's Hospice totals £2,342, stage lighting for the village £607 and for The Friends of St. Peter's Church £245 – not a bad effort for a small village.

A Miscellany of Music & Mirth – 10th & 11th September 2010
Back row: *Martin Stockley, John Cottrell, Keith Moore, Russen Thomas, Michael Cooper, Roger Marshall, Roger Poole,*
Middle row: *Gareth MacLatchy, Tim Wyatt, Steve Herbert, Sandra Lee, Laurian Cooper, Kathryn King, Heather Cottrell, Jean Marshall, Lynne Moore*
Front row: *Jo Harrison, Sarah Nutt, Marjorie Stockley, Duncan Hughes, Wendy Thomas, Lyn Wyatt, Sally Pritchard*

Chapter 11 – ROYAL CELEBRATIONS

The village would have come together to mark these occasions just as we prepare now for this year's Diamond Jubilee.

Queen Victoria Diamond Jubilee – June 1897
King Edward VII Coronation – August 1902
King George V Coronation – June 1911
King George V & Queen Mary Silver Jubilee – May 1935
King George VI Coronation – May 1937
Queen Elizabeth II Coronation – 1953
Queen Elizabeth II Silver Jubilee – 1977
Queen Elizabeth II Golden Jubilee – 2002
Queen Elizabeth II Diamond Jubilee – 2012 – our queen is only the 2nd British monarch to celebrate a Diamond Jubilee – the first being Queen Victoria.

From an article by Rev. W.L. Jones (vicar 1955-60) published in the Parish Magazine:

The village had a splendid meat tea to celebrate the Coronation of Edward VII in 1902 – 2 legs of mutton, 2 hams each of 15lbs, 2 joints of beef each 30lbs, 30lbs corned beef, 36 dozen halfpenny buns, 10lbs of cheese, 100lbs cake, 12 dozen lemonade, 12 dozen ginger beer at a shilling per gallon. Two ladies were paid for washing up.

Photo taken outside Springwood – the Vicarage c 1901/2 – among the earliest photos we have of an assembled group. Far left: Mr. H. Davies school master. Seated centre the Reverend C.H. Luxton with dog. Everyone is dressed in their Sunday best so possibly a Sunday School celebration or could they be about to celebrate Edward VII's coronation and enjoy the aforementioned tea?

SilverJubilee of King George V

On the 6th May 1935 the village celebrated the Silver Jubilee of King George V and Queen Mary in great style.

The Wellington Weekly News :

Langford Budville's Great Day

The Jubilee day opened with a peal on the Church bells, the ringers continuing their work at intervals throughout the day. At 9.45 there was a well attended and inspiring service at the Church. At 2.00pm the parishioners gathered at the highest point on Langford Heathfield for the opening of the permanent memorial – a massive seat on concrete uprights, the work of local craftsmen. The vicar (Rev. S.J.S. Swainson) who was accompanied by Mr. T. Fox (chairman of the committee), Mr & Mrs C.L. Forster and the churchwardens (Messrs J. Bunny and W.S.Braddick), said the occasion was felt to be an opportune one in which to pay a tribute of respect and affection to Mr Albert Stone, whom he asked to unveil the memorial. Mr. Stone, now 85, had throughout his life been devoted to all that concerned the welfare of the village. Mr. Stone, after the unveiling replied in fitting terms and called for 3 cheers for the King…A move was then made to Langford Court, where by the kindness of Mr & Mrs Van Heusen, a series of attractions and games took place, which lasted until the late evening. A band, conducted by Mr Van Heusen, added to the gaiety of the occasion. The programme consisted of fancy dress parade for children, Maypole dances and Tableaux, and the games provided were skittles, the Greasy Pole and Pole Sparring. From 4-6 p.m. the whole village were entertained to tea at the Village Hall, in three relays. At 10.00pm a beacon fire, about 25ft high built at the highest point of the Heathfield (400ft) was kindled by Mrs Van Heusen (Langford Court). The tower of the Church was also floodlit under the direction of Mr. T. Fox…At 8.00pm the King's broadcast speech was listened to and at 9.15pm Mr. Fox proposed a vote of thanks to all those who had cooperated in achieving the success of the day… Jubilee mugs were presented to all the school children of the village by Mr & Mrs C.L. Forster of Wellisford Manor.

Melvyn Jones is dressed as a knave standing by the shoulder of the seated bearded man – possibly Albert Stone

Named here are Albert Hayes, Eileen (nee Perry) Wotton, Bill Holway and Margie Salway, Fred Salway, Reg Stone, Robert Stone, Annie Broom

The photographs show the gathering for the unveiling of the Silver Jubilee Seat, made by Ernest Jones, carpenter and wheelwright with ironwork probably by Charlie Wood, blacksmith. It still commands a position on the edge of the common for all to enjoy the fantastic view across to the Quantocks although unfortunately the view the other way to Haddon Hill is now obscured by trees.

This year 2012 a Diamond Jubilee seat will be unveiled which will be situated at the western edge of the Triangle looking over towards the Blackdown Hills.

King George VI Coronation

Rose Cottage decorated for George VI Coronation 1937 – home of Fred & Jin Salway

Queen Elizabeth II Coronation

Roger Wotton remembers celebrating Queen Elizabeth II's coronation with a party in the field opposite what is now White Post Nursery, and the presentation of a blue glass Coronation mug which he still has. John Cottrell also remembers that all the children sent off a balloon with their name and address on it to see whose would go the furthest.

Blue glass Coronation mug

Queen's Silver Jubilee & Golden Jubilee

Gerald Brewer recalls:

Queen's Silver Jubilee
A project committee under the auspices of the Parish Council organised, in the afternoon, a Fete in the grounds and barn at the Martlet Inn. Teas were supplied from the Martlet kitchen by mine hosts Gwyn and Pete Harris and there was a special tea party and fancy dress parade for the children who were all presented with a celebration medal. In the evening there was a BBQ held in the orchard and car park of the Martlet with an outdoor skittle competition actually in the orchard. It was a huge success as great numbers came.

Queen's Golden Jubilee

The village was trimmed with bunting and on the Sunday evening Reverend David Randall held Songs of Praise in the Churchyard. On the Monday the road through the village was closed from Croxhall to the Crossroads and there was a street fair with a variety of stalls positioned along the way. A children's tea party followed in the afternoon and the children were presented with celebration mugs by Mrs Penny Lloyd. Lunches were served by members of the Church in the Martlet and Friends of the Langford Budville School had a BBQ in the road serving hot dogs. In the evening there was a hog roast and the entertainment was the Wurzels Country Dance Band in the barn at Bere Farm. All the events were organised as before by a sub-committee of the Parish Council.

Queen's Diamond Jubilee

History is about to repeat itself for the Queen's Diamond Jubilee when there is an exciting programme of events organised under the auspices of the Langford Budville and Runnington Parish Council – sub-committee under the experienced guidance of Gerald Brewer – with the support and cooperation of the Church and Village Hall Management Committee:

Thursday 31st May
2.00pm   Diamond Jubilee Tea Party at the Village School for the children and a few invited guests
Saturday 2nd June
A choice of 3 free guided walks starting and finishing at Langford Lakes with refreshments available after the walks at 4.00pm
9.30am 15 miles with lunch stop at the Globe, Appley (bring packed lunch or pre-book at the Globe). Mainly level, two steep hills
11.00am 10miles. Footpaths and bridleways within Langford Budville parish. Suitable for regular walkers. Packed lunch required
2.00pm 2-3 miles. Family walk through Langford Heathfield and rolling hills and fields. Not suitable for buggies. Well behaved dogs welcome on all walks. Routes may be changed subject to weather conditions. Donation towards cost of refreshments if desired. Further details from Zenah Rowe
6.00pm Music and entertainment at Springwood by kind permission of Chris and Flora Bartlett. Bring your own picnic
Tickets £6.00 (proceeds to St. Peter's Church) from Wendy Thomas or Lyn Wyatt
Sunday 3rd June
9.15am Service at St. Peter's Church followed by tree planting ceremony in Churchyard at 10.30am (tree donated by the Woodland Trust). Refreshments afterwards in the church
10.30am Jubilee family service at Runnington Church, followed by picnic lunch
Monday 4th June
11.00am Open air service and unveiling of the new Jubilee seat on the Triangle
12.00 noon Family fun football match and picnic lunch on the Triangle
3.00pm Presentation of Commemorative Jubilee Mugs at the Village School followed by children's tea party
6.00pm Sing-along, followed by hog roast and barn dance at Langford Lakes. Free to all residents of Langford Budvlle and Runnington. Family friends welcome for a small donation

In addition to the above events organised by the parish sub-committee, The Martlet will have a celebratory evening on Friday 1st June, with a supper of fish and chips or sausage and mash followed by a sing-along for all to join in.

A final event takes place at the Martlet Inn at 1.00pm on Tuesday 5th June (an extra Bank Holiday); the Book Launch of *Changing Faces* – published to commemorate Her Majesty Queen Elizabeth II Diamond Jubilee June 2012

Chapter 12 – STILL CHANGING FACES – SOME FINAL THOUGHTS...

Everyday life in the village has changed fundamentally over the past 100 years or so. Until the coming of the motor-car and buses people relied on horses, Shanks's pony and bicycles (when they came into being and if they could afford them) in order to get them to nearby places like Milverton, Wiveliscombe, Wellington and Taunton. So the village had to be self-sufficient and the 19th century censuses show that, in addition to occupations connected to the land such as blacksmiths, wheelwrights and numerous agricultural labourers, Langford Budville also contained tailors, thatchers, shoemakers, dressmakers, washerwomen, hat-makers (particularly straw), carpenters, and a butcher, as well as other shop- and inn-keepers. While most people worked on the land some earned a wage from the wool factory at Wellington founded by the We(a)re family, related by marriage to the Foxes. These families were highly successful Quaker industrial entrepreneurs introducing good practices, such as sick pay and a pension scheme, for their employees. The woollen industry formed an important part of the history of the area emanating from excellent pasture for sheep, fast running streams and a skilled workforce.

Horses played a central role well into the 20th century in agriculture, brewing, mail, transport of goods to and from market, the doctor on his rounds and in recreation. As roads improved, public horse-drawn services, then railways, canals and bus services came into being and provided opportunities for those who were inclined to venture to 'foreign parts' beyond the village. As ownership of the motor car became more prevalent, people increasingly sought work beyond the village and nowadays most people travel out of the village to work.

For those who could read, the coming of newspapers helped them to learn about the world 'beyond'. The *Wellington Weekly News* was established in 1860 and in its early days reported national and international news, not just the local happenings. The Post Office was the communication hub for incoming and outgoing correspondence – and for catching up with the local gossip. Within living memory it was run, at one time, by two rather portly ladies. They drove an Austin 7 and in order to even out the weight one of them had to sit diagonally behind whoever was driving!! Gerald Brewer remembers going with his dad to shoot rabbits at the weekend. He would then take a brace to the ladies in exchange for 5 Woodbines or 10 Players Weights.

The advent of the wireless kept people abreast of world affairs. Heavy battery accumulators were used and Gerald recalls having to take accumulators to Sam Crowcombe at 2 Heathfield who in turn took them to his brother Fred in Runnington for re-charging. People remember with great fondness Sam's wife Elsie Crowcombe delivering milk in all weathers. She pushed around a make-shift pram-like cart and dispensed milk with a ladle.

Everyone baked, bottled and preserved fruits and vegetables as they came into season. Food for the average family consisted of potatoes, bread, rabbits and home-grown vegetables. Most made their own bread, jam and dripping. Many kept their own chickens and during the 2nd World War if you kept chickens you didn't get a ration book with

*Tom Perry with Frank Gage –
Stancombe Farm c1961/62*

coupons for eggs – instead you got coupons to buy meal to feed the chickens. Pigs were a major source of meat both for farming families and others who kept a pig or two in the back yard. Charlie Wood, the village blacksmith 1930-70, was apparently the keeper of the village boar – the sty is still visible behind the Old Forge.

Open fires used to burn most rubbish. Newspapers and wood were used for lighting fires, bonfires burnt garden waste and vegetables scraps/leftovers were fed to pigs or chickens. That was of course until the invention of plastic! Doing the washing used to be a whole day's work. Not much has been reported about the Depression years but one can only suppose that people living off the land were luckier than those in towns and cities. Some people of course emigrated in search of a better life.

Seasons dictated the pattern of people's farming lives – sowing in spring, haymaking in early summer followed by planting of root crops and harvesting grains in late summer. Until mechanisation, farming was very labour intensive as can be seen by the censuses with a large proportion of people working as agricultural labourers.

Just as an aside, a story goes that Robert 'Bob' Perry (Tom's dad) used to go with his horse and trap into Wellington on a Saturday night to drink at the Ship Inn. After a jolly evening the horse would bring him home! There were no drinking and driving laws then to worry about.

*William H. Brewer
centre back and Ernest
Tucker right with
fellow farm workers at
Middle Chipley Farm
c 1940*

In the 1940s tractors and other machinery had a huge effect on agricultural practices and particularly the number of men required. At the same time, the need for smiths and wheelwrights gradually declined. In 1957 a Parliamentary Act encouraged the removal of hedges to create bigger fields for larger machines; this heralded the demise of the patchwork landscape of small fields although it did give farmers the opportunity to increase productivity.

Until the 2nd World War orchards were an important part of village livelihood. They have largely disappeared through neglect or for economic reasons. Production of cider was an essential part of the farming regime as workers on the land usually consumed half a gallon per day!

The village never had its own doctor and relied on doctors visiting from Wellington – names remembered were Dr. Harding who drove an old Bentley, and Dr. Johnston. When Gerald Brewer was about to arrive in this world his dad had to cycle to Nynehead to fetch the District Nurse. There was also an obvious difficulty in contacting the fire-brigade in Wellington before the advent of telephones and many old thatched cottages burned down – or were condemned as insanitary. How different things are now as most people have a telephone and/or mobile phone and the village telephone box is no more.

Piped water, electricity and automated machinery all helped to ease the drudgery of former times. Electricity was first brought to the village in the late 20's and early 30's. Some people remember their parents saying that it was in place by 1935 for those who could afford it. Most people were connected by the 1950s. Before that of course people used oil lamps or candles. In 1951 there was a proposal to bring mains sewerage to the village; until then most houses had septic tanks or cesspits.

The demise of the village telephone box

It would appear that water in this particular area was and has continued to be plentiful. Our research has indicated that there were wells situated at:

- Old Post/St.Peter's Cottage (there was once a public house here)
- Courtlands Farm – one well was down by the stream and used to supply North and South Gundenham. Apparently it still supplies the cattle with drinking water at South Gundenham. In the 60s Jim Cottrell laid mains from Bere Farm to Gundenham. North Gundenham now has its own bore hole. South Gundenham still has a 15' well in the courtyard with an old Victorian pump.
- Behind no 3 Rose Cottages
- Near what are now Chapel View cottages (there was once a public house next door)

- At Three Ashes, where Coppins and the Wedge now stand.
- End of Chorwell Lane – there was apparently a 4 inch iron pipe laid by the Sanford Estate in a very straight line from there all the way to Nynehead, feeding Nynehead as well as Hornsey Farm en route, and it is still in use.
- Wellsmead – an underground well/tank fed by spring water used to supply most of the village. It is believed that this source of water comes all the way from the Black Mountains in Wales (by way of confirmation, Oake Manor Golf Club claims this to be the source of its own well water).
- A 300' deep bore hole at the cement block house opposite White Post Nurseries which used to supply Gundenham and half of the village is no longer in use - it was originally put in by the Sanford Estate in c1910. It had a huge storage tank on the roof and was complete with an old lift pump.
- A well was at one time located under what is now Sliema's drive, and used by Cload Cottages, of which only Brockney House remains.
- There would almost certainly have been a well at the Martlet but the location is not clear. (When the cellar floods it is because it is below the level of the road, not due to the exact location of a well)
- All the local farms, usually built in low places because of the need to provide water for cattle, would have had a well/pump/water supply. A number of wells were built by the Sanford Estate on farmland and were very well constructed. The majority are now buried.

Gerald Brewer remembers as a boy in the 50's fetching water from the Chorwell Lane well. He also remembers the Pulsford water bowser coming into the village when water was scarce on a hot summer's day. With the building of Clatworthy reservoir in 1958 mains water supply came to the whole of the village and still comes via the waterworks station at Bere Farm.

In living memory the village had a blacksmith, wheel-wright/undertaker, post-office, shops, and a chapel. None of these has survived, but it still has a pub, school and a church. There was a shop – general stores one assumes – at what is now Chapel View in the house of William H. Brewer, Valerie Pitman's grandfather, where she can particularly remember him making ice cream to sell – what small child would not? Another shop was located in Copplestones in the home of Frank Salway. People remember Bertha Leatt in a small shop selling sweets and crisps in the then Courtlands Farm. Post is still delivered daily but the sight of the postman and post van might soon become a thing of the past as more and more people 'go on line'. How much longer will people have newspapers and/or milk delivered to their doorstep before breakfast? Shopping has changed so much today with supermarkets a short car drive or bus ride away and vans delivering direct to homes with orders being made on mobile phones or the internet.

The village is still home to a number of commercial enterprises. Already mentioned in the book are The Martlet Inn and the Bindon House Hotel. In addition are:

Langford Lakes Christmas Tree Farm – ' family run 40 acre farm since 1971 owned and run by Reg Hendy with help from his wife Ann and sons Shaun and Nick. Initially farming wheat and potatoes, the next enterprise from 1978 to 2000 was an Agricultural Engineering Business, employing two people, serving the local farming community. The primary business is now Christmas Trees – Nordman Firs – established in 1993. Coarse fishing is also on offer with day and season passes on any of the four fishing lakes, which were stocked in 1980.'

Reg and Ann Hendy with sons Nick and Shaun

Deane Barton Egg Farm – 'fresh local free-range farm eggs'

Willis & Grabham – 'chainsaw and garden machinery specialists offering sales, service and repairs.'

White Post Nursery – 'selling a selection of unusual and unique plants as well as old favourites. In the summer a teashop serves cream teas and cakes.'

Wellie Cabs – 'courteous local cab company.'

Gundenham Dairies – 'established over 80 years and home of some of the finest locally produced milk and dairy produce in Somerset.'

Langford Budville has metamorphosed over the years to meet the demands of the day. The skyline has changed as new buildings have replaced old ones and new developments have taken place. The village population of around 300 has however probably remained fairly constant for several hundred years. Most would agree that it is a special place to live, situated as it is in a picturesque part of the West Somerset countryside. The views from the village are extensive, taking in the Quantocks, the Blackdowns and on a fine day the Polden Hills. A short drive of 2 miles brings you to the 'Food Town' of Wellington with a very good selection of shops. The county town of Taunton and all it has to offer is also easily accessible, within a 20-25 minute drive. The M5 motorway is ten minutes away and even the seaside is easily accessible – 12 miles to St. Audries on the north Somerset coast and 23 miles to Sidmouth on the south Devon coast. I'm beginning to sound like an estate agent but sometimes it is important to reflect how lucky we are. Throughout the years the inhabitants of the village have been the custodians of the future – just as we are now. So thank you to all those who have gone before us and helped to make the village what it is today.

EPILOGUE

Roger Wotton

I was born into the village two years after the end of the Second World War, a year before the National Health Service existed and unaware that it was a country in the grip of food rationing. Village men returned from countries they had never heard of, or even knew where they had been. Some never returned.

How the villagers were affected by the hardship of war and rationing is hard to tell, as my childhood memory shows me pictures of gardens laid to vegetable production, with little favour to the lawns and flowers that dominate the gardens in 2012. Men would return home in the evenings to work in the garden until daylight disappeared, although digging by the light of a hurricane lamp was not uncommon.

It was a time of simple pleasures; few, if any houses had inside toilets, bath tubs hung on the back walls, radios were valve driven, music came from hand wound gramophones, televisions had been heard of but not seen. The church was the village and the village was the church. The rhythm of village life revolved around Christian festivals and the seasons of the year. Fetes were held on the lawns of the vicarage and dances in the Men's Working Club. Sixty years ago a village party took place in the fields to celebrate the coronation of Queen Elizabeth II and a blue glass Coronation Mug was given to every village child; though faded and marked through use as a flower vase, it still stands in my cabinet.

The common land was the village back garden, children played on the heath and in the woods, without fear of strangers or safety; if there was a tree, it had to be climbed. The time for returning home was marked only by the passage of the sun and the striking of the church clock, not by a mobile phone.

The weather forecast was read in the skies, bad weather meant extra clothing, not staying at home, and I am sure it snowed every year.

Children grow into adults and move away.

I have been gone many a year, but when my course is run, I will return. I will walk the paths of childhood, but not leave a footprint, I will watch village life and the seasons pass, but not be seen, I will again ring the church bell but not pull the rope, I will join in the hymns of praise, but not be heard, I will rest in the soil of Langford and be content, for I am but a note on a page of history.

My grateful thanks to Marjorie Stockley and all involved in this wonderful venture of chronicling the life of Langford Budville which has reunited me with friends and family, some not seen in over fifty years.

POST SCRIPT

'To make an end is to make a beginning and the end is where we start from'
T.S. Eliot

The book does not purport to be the final word on Langford Budville's past but just the beginning. It is hoped that others will be encouraged to discover more and more about this very special corner of West Somerset.

There are two regrets:

1) That as time was of the essence we had to curtail our research but there is much more detail about Langford Budville still to be discovered.

2) That we were unable to expand our research much beyond the village of Langford Budville – there is little historical detail included in the book of Wellisford, Runnington or Middle Chipley, although they are all part of the Parish of Langford Budville. Maybe in the fullness of time this can be remedied. As we go to press Runnington is setting up a History group, which is exciting news. We wish them well in their pursuit and look forward to reading all their findings one day.

As the new girl on the block, having only lived here for four years, I will undoubtedly have omitted some crucial facts and made some wrong assertions for which I can only apologise. I have wherever possible tried to verify the information through primary and secondary sources. In the event of the book being reprinted at any time in the future I would be grateful for any amendments in writing to mastock@globalnet.co.uk or 5 Courtlands, Langford Budville TA21 0BF.

ACKNOWLEDGEMENTS 2012
For their many varied but vital contributions

Stuart Anderson
Iain Beath
Vic Biggs
Carolyn Bill
Neil & Amy Blackmore
Mike & Maggie Blake
Gerald & Ann Brewer
Sue Brewer
Margaret & David Brown
Terena Burgess & Bruno Fellman
Ann Case
Laurian & Michael Cooper
David, Sue & Helen Cottrell
Heather & John Cottrell
Sarah Davies – the Diocese of Bath & Wells
Joy Eady
Christopher Fox
Clemency Fox
Lorna Gibbs
Sylvia & Philip Gothard
Sheena Griffiths
Anne Harris
Kathryn Harris
John & Pam Harries
Robert Hayes
William Hayes
Steve & Cherry Herbert
Duncan & Rachel Hughes
Lyn Jaffa
Glyn Jones
S W Kenyon
Langford Budville & Runnington Churches
  Parish Magazine
Langford Budville Residents' Association
  for their generous donation
Barbara Lawrence
John & Sandra Lawrence
Limited Edition
John Lloyd MC
Richard & Jane Lloyd
Ian Loudon – voluntary warden –
  Langford Heathfield
David Mainhood
Jean & Roger Marshall
June Marshall
Mark Brian McDermott – Historian
Lynne & Keith Moore
Sarah Nutt

David Percy
Jenny Perry-Jones
Wendy & Ronald Phillips
Bute Pike
Valerie Pitman
Roger Poole

Mr. David Rabsan – Nynehead History
  Society
Joyce Randall
Janet Read

Colleen Sanders
Mr. K. Sharpe – Headmaster –
  Langford Budville, Church of England
  Primary School
Heather Schefe – Queensland, Australia
Colin Spackman, Museum &
  Local History Society – Wellington
Betty Sparks
Dr. Amelia Stockley
Martin Stockley
John Stone

Wendy & Russen Thomas
Sue Toomey
Carol Tucker
Alan Tucker

Tony Verrier – Somerset County Council

Wellington Weekly News

Chris Widdows
Dr Graham & Gill Wilson
Sally Woods
Roger Wotton
Lyn & Tim Wyatt

Present day photography – particular thanks
to David Brown, Jean & Roger Marshall,
Keith Moore, Laighton Waymouth and
Martin Stockley.

To all those listed and any inadvertently
omitted my grateful thanks

BIBLIOGRAPHY

Ten Hides – A Millennial History of Fitzhead, Somerset - Adrian Cross
Stained Glass & the Victorian Gothic Revival – Jim Cheshire
A People Bewitched - Davies
Blame it on the Vicar - Evans
History of Milverton – Frank E. Farley & Don F. Ekless
Wiveliscombe – A History – Susan Maria Farrington & the Wiveliscombe Book Group
The Grand Western Canal – a brief history by Helen Harris
Materials for the History of Wellington – Humphreys
Rise & Fall of Merry England – Ronald Hutton
Wellington Through Time – Douglas Marshall
1973 The Administration of the Poor Law in the Somerset Parish of Langford Budville during 1657-1730 & 1782-1836 - Mark Mc Dermott
Langford Court – Mark Mc Dermott
PoorLaw/Manor House/Church House – Mark Mc Dermott
The Book of Nynehead – Nynehead & District Local History Society
Somerset Archaeological Society – Terry Pearson
Bindon Estate – notes on the history – Julia Small
A Study of Rural Settlement in Somerset by Beatrice Swainson
History of Taunton – Wickenden
The Somerset Home Guard – a pictorial roll-call - Jeffery Wilson
Wellington Weekly News - microfiche at Somerset Heritage Centre
Medieval Wellington – Bruce Watkin
Wellington & the Civil War – Gordon Woodbury

With thanks to the Somerset Heritage Centre with its plethora of
material relating to Langford Budville both in the archives and
on the shelves – too numerous to record.

FAMILY TREES

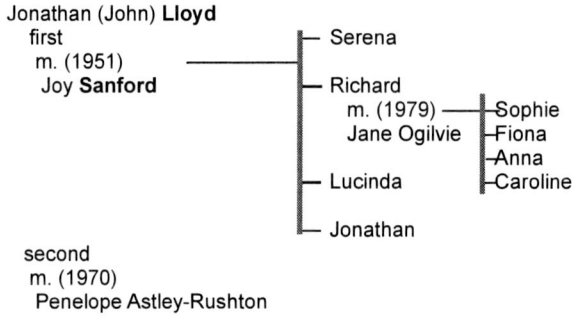

Jonathan (John) **Lloyd**
first
m. (1951)
Joy **Sanford**

— Serena

— Richard
　m. (1979) —— Sophie
　Jane Ogilvie —Fiona
　　　　　　　—Anna
　　　　　　　—Caroline

— Lucinda

— Jonathan

second
m. (1970)
Penelope Astley-Rushton

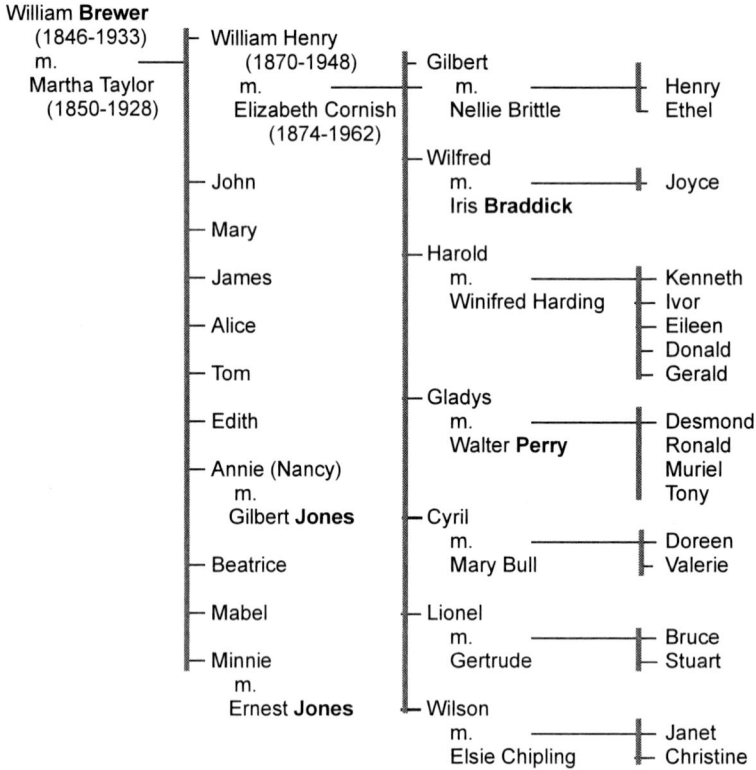

William **Brewer**
(1846-1933)
m.
Martha Taylor
(1850-1928)

— William Henry
　(1870-1948)
　m.
　Elizabeth Cornish
　(1874-1962)

— John

— Mary

— James

— Alice

— Tom

— Edith

— Annie (Nancy)
　m.
　Gilbert **Jones**

— Beatrice

— Mabel

— Minnie
　m.
　Ernest **Jones**

— Gilbert
　m.
　Nellie Brittle
　　　— Henry
　　　— Ethel

— Wilfred
　m.
　Iris **Braddick**
　　　— Joyce

— Harold
　m.
　Winifred Harding
　　　— Kenneth
　　　— Ivor
　　　— Eileen
　　　— Donald
　　　— Gerald

— Gladys
　m.
　Walter **Perry**
　　　— Desmond
　　　　Ronald
　　　　Muriel
　　　　Tony

— Cyril
　m.
　Mary Bull
　　　— Doreen
　　　— Valerie

— Lionel
　m.
　Gertrude
　　　— Bruce
　　　— Stuart

— Wilson
　m.
　Elsie Chipling
　　　— Janet
　　　— Christine

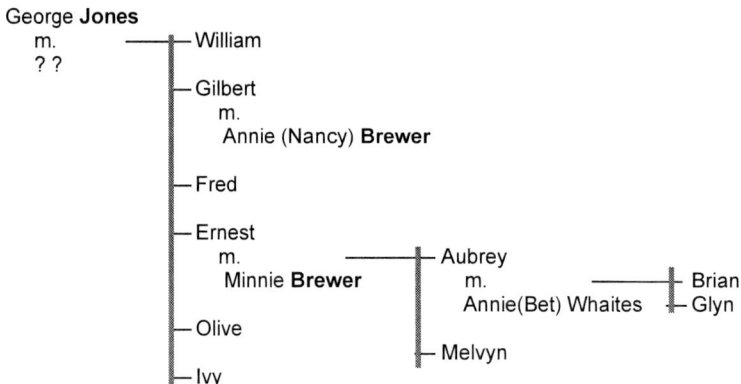

George **Jones**
m.
? ?

— William

— Gilbert
　m.
　Annie (Nancy) **Brewer**

— Fred

— Ernest
　m.
　Minnie **Brewer**
　　　— Aubrey
　　　　m.
　　　　Annie(Bet) Whaites
　　　　　— Brian
　　　　　— Glyn

　　　— Melvyn

— Olive

— Ivy

Salway – Watson – Perry – Wotton

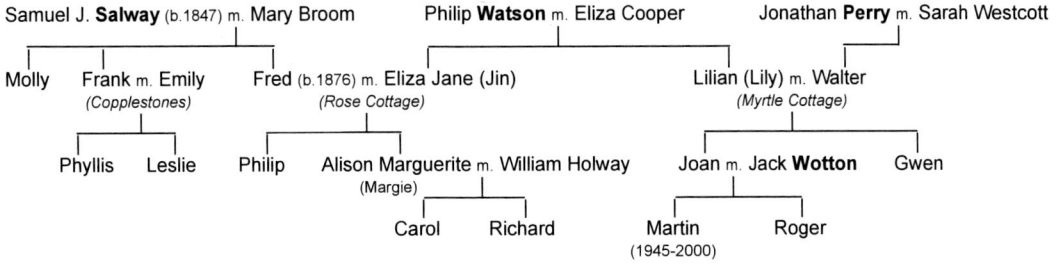

Samuel J. **Salway** (b.1847) m. Mary Broom   Philip **Watson** m. Eliza Cooper   Jonathan **Perry** m. Sarah Westcott

Molly   Frank m. Emily   Fred (b.1876) m. Eliza Jane (Jin)   Lilian (Lily) m. Walter
        (Copplestones)   *(Rose Cottage)*   *(Myrtle Cottage)*

Phyllis   Leslie   Philip   Alison Marguerite m. William Holway   Joan m. Jack **Wotton**   Gwen
                                      (Margie)

Carol   Richard   Martin   Roger
                          (1945-2000)

James **Hayes**
m. (1909)
Mary Anne Greedy

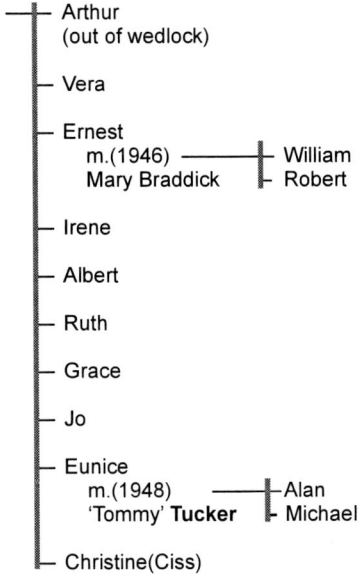

— Arthur
  (out of wedlock)

— Vera

— Ernest
    m.(1946) ——— William
    Mary Braddick — Robert

— Irene

— Albert

— Ruth

— Grace

— Jo

— Eunice
    m.(1948) ——— Alan
    'Tommy' **Tucker** — Michael

— Christine(Ciss)

William V. **Braddick**
      (1860-?)
  m. ———
Fanny Hatcher
  (1879-?)

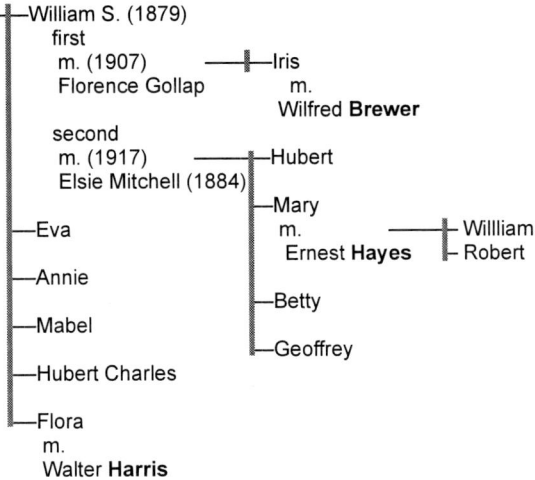

— William S. (1879)
    first
    m. (1907) ——— Iris
    Florence Gollap   m.
                     Wilfred **Brewer**

    second
    m. (1917) ——— Hubert
    Elsie Mitchell (1884)
                  — Mary
                    m. ——— Willliam
                    Ernest **Hayes** — Robert

                  — Betty

                  — Geoffrey

— Eva

— Annie

— Mabel

— Hubert Charles

— Flora
    m.
  Walter **Harris**

Appendix B
Listed Buildings/Monuments in parish of Langford Budville

	Grade
Bindon House (Now Bindon House Hotel)	2
Church of St. Peter, Langford Budville	1
Church of St. Peter, Runnington	2*
Cloth finishing works, Tone Mills, North Range	2*
Dunn's Farmhouse	2
Fursdons inc. Chipley Barn to N.E.(Ash, beech and oak barns)	2
Harpford Bridge	2
Harpford Farmhouse	2
Higher Wellisford	2
Hillview Cottages & Walls returned to central porch	2
Langford Court	2*
Remains of Cross 3 m S of porch, St. Peter's Church	2
Road Bridge at NGR ST 1077 2132	2
Runnington House	2
Stancombe Farmhouse	2
The Old Coach House (formerly part of Wellisford Manor)	2
The Old Vicarage, Langford Budville	2
Unidentified tomb 1 m E of south porch, St. Peter's Church	2
Unidentified tomb 1 m W of south porch, St. Peter's Church	2
Unidentified tomb 2 m NE of chancel, St. Peter's Church	2
Warehouse 25 m W. Harpford Bridge FH (Harpford Mill)	2
Wellisford Manor	2

Grade 1 buildings of exceptional interest, sometimes considered to be internationally important
Grade 2* particularly important buildings of more than special interest
Grade 2 buildings that are 'nationally important and of special interest.
Taken from tauntondeane.gov.uk website

Appendix C
Langford Budville Parish Council 2012

The parish council has responsibility for local issues, including setting an annual precept(local rate) to cover the council's operating costs and producing annual accounts for public scrutiny. The parish council evaluates local planning applications and works with local police, district council officers, and neighbourhood watch groups on matters of crime, security and traffic. The parish council's role also includes initiating projects for the maintenance, repair, and improvement of highways, drainage, footpaths, public transport, and street cleaning. Conservation matters (including trees and listed buildings) and environmental issues are also the responsibility of the council.

Chairman	Mr. J. Cottrell
Vice-chairman	Mr. G. Brewer
Clerk to the Council	Mrs G. Hake

Mr. R. Hendy Mr. K. McGrath Mr. R. Poole

Appendix D

GEOLOGY AND LANDSCAPE
Keith Moore MA PGCE CGeol FGS

Imagine Somerset with a desert climate of strong dry winds whipping up sandstorms and building dunes, interrupted from time to time by torrential downpours leading to flash floods, carrying huge quantities of sediment of all shapes and sizes, depositing it eventually in temporary lakes where crystals of gypsum and other minerals formed as the water evaporated.

Difficult to imagine? These were the conditions during the Permian and Triassic periods around 260– 210 million years ago when the strata underlying Langford Budville today were formed. The Triassic world would have been unrecognisable to us; the British Isles was near the centre of a supercontinent named Laurasia, consisting of North America, Europe and Asia, before the Atlantic Ocean existed. Somerset lay about 25 degrees North of the Equator at this time. Langford Budville is now situated on latitude 51°N and longitude 3°16'W.

The strata laid deposited in this area have two common characteristics. Firstly they are coloured red (indeed the beds were once referred to as the New Red Sandstone) and secondly they are almost completely devoid of fossils. Both characteristics are a direct result of the depositional environment at the time. The redness is due to the hot semi-arid climate causing iron minerals to become oxidised and form a coating on every sand grain and pebble. The lack of fossils reflects the harshness of the environment which would have made habitation very difficult and the likelihood of fossilisation remote.

The rock types underlying Langford Budville vary from fine mudstones (sometimes called marls) with evaporate minerals, through cross bedded sandstones to coarse conglomerates and breccias (with rounded or angular pebbles respectively). This range of types reflects the variability of depositional environments both in space and time and combined with the lack of fossils makes subdividing and correlating the strata very difficult. As a result there is a plethora of local rock names and only a broad division into recognisable units (fig. 1). The outcrop pattern (fig. 2) reflects the fact that the strata are tilted gently to the South East and therefore become progressively younger in that direction.

The beds vary considerably in their resistance to weathering and erosion and in their permeability. Generally the pebble and boulder beds form higher ground while the mudstones are more easily eroded and form lower, less well drained areas, for example much of Langford Heathfield. Many of the coarser beds are permeable and form localised springs where they sit above less permeable mudstones. Some of these have proved reliable enough to provide a water supply, as illustrated by the spring north of Ritherdon's Lane which once fed parts of the village. In other areas shallow boreholes drilled into the coarser units have provided reliable supplies, for example at North Gundenham. The sandstone and pebble beds form light well drained soils which historically were suitable for arable farming while the mudstones formed soils more suitable for pasture, though modern agricultural practice has probably made this distinction less clear today.

A further complication to the outcrop pattern is that the strata have been subjected to earth moving forces since they were laid down and as well as being gently tilted, they are extensively fractured. Many of the fractures are actually faults showing considerable displacement (which would incidentally have generated earthquakes at the time – fortunately many millions of years ago). The faults have the effect of bringing different rock types into contact with each other. The resultant landscape is a combination of the South East dip, faulting and the variety of rock types, combined with prolonged erosion, though the effects are now mostly too subtle to be easily definable.

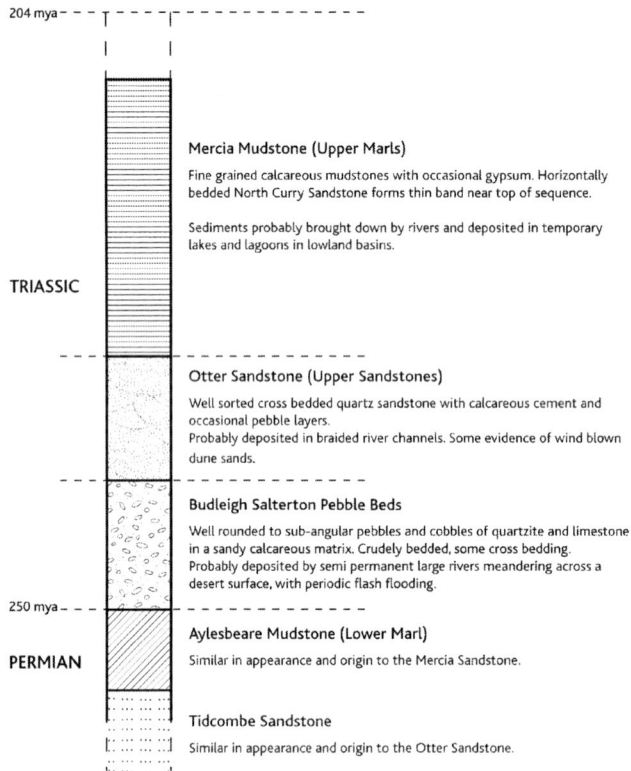

204 mya

Mercia Mudstone (Upper Marls)
Fine grained calcareous mudstones with occasional gypsum. Horizontally bedded North Curry Sandstone forms thin band near top of sequence.

Sediments probably brought down by rivers and deposited in temporary lakes and lagoons in lowland basins.

TRIASSIC

Otter Sandstone (Upper Sandstones)
Well sorted cross bedded quartz sandstone with calcareous cement and occasional pebble layers.
Probably deposited in braided river channels. Some evidence of wind blown dune sands.

Budleigh Salterton Pebble Beds
Well rounded to sub-angular pebbles and cobbles of quartzite and limestone in a sandy calcareous matrix. Crudely bedded, some cross bedding.
Probably deposited by semi permanent large rivers meandering across a desert surface, with periodic flash flooding.

250 mya

Aylesbeare Mudstone (Lower Marl)
Similar in appearance and origin to the Mercia Sandstone.

PERMIAN

Tidcombe Sandstone
Similar in appearance and origin to the Otter Sandstone.

Fig. 1 Geological succession underlying Langford Budville
Based on BGS sheet 311 Wellington 2009 by permission of the British Geological Survey. All rights reserved

Eventually the Triassic desert landscape was submerged beneath the sea and younger strata were deposited on top of the eroded land surface. Later earth movements raised these strata above sea level and over Langford Budville they have been completely eroded away. They are however well displayed as the Upper Greensand of the Blackdown Hills a few km. to the South. These almost horizontal Cretaceous strata are said to rest unconformably on the tilted and faulted Triassic beds underneath (fig. 3). The Greensand provided a tough building stone called Chert (a very finely crystalline silica rich rock) but little of this has found its way down to Langford Budville though there just might be a Greensand whetstone lurking in the back of a garden shed somewhere in the village.

Numerous small disused quarries dot the landscape around the village. On the basis that stone was difficult to transport over any distance, most vernacular architecture made use of local resources and undoubtedly many of the quarries yielded building stone. The quality is however variable; at their best some of the sandstones form good building material, easily worked and resistant to weathering. The coarser beds fare less well but have nevertheless been extensively utilised. A few moments studying the walls of St Peter's church will reveal both the variety of rock types and the variations in weathering resistance. Two polished slabs of the Pebble Beds can be seen in the chancel, providing an excellent opportunity to study the variety of sizes, shapes and lithologies of the included pebbles. The church also contains two other notable rock types; most of the interior stonework together with windows and door frames is Ham Hill Stone, a Jurassic limestone which is easily dressed and carved, while the coping stones on the churchyard wall are North Curry Sandstone, a tough Late Triassic rock probably formed in shallow water and notable among Triassic rocks for its lack of redness. It may have been quarried near Norton Fitzwarren. The Mercia Mudstones in particular were suitable for brick making and though there is no direct evidence of this in the village itself, the red bricks made at Poole near Wellington can also be found in many buildings in the village.

Key to Figures 2 & 3

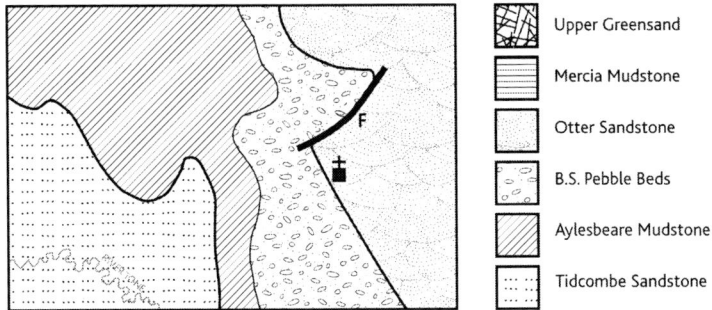

Fig. 2 Geological sketch map

Upper Greensand

Mercia Mudstone

Otter Sandstone

B.S. Pebble Beds

Aylesbeare Mudstone

Tidcombe Sandstone

1 KM

A glance at a map will also reveal lime kilns adjacent to some of the quarries (for example beside the footpath opposite Bere Farm). Lime was a vital agricultural and constructional commodity and was derived from burning limestone in the kilns. There are no pure limestones in the Triassic strata under the village. However some of the conglomerates contain high concentrations of Carboniferous limestone pebbles

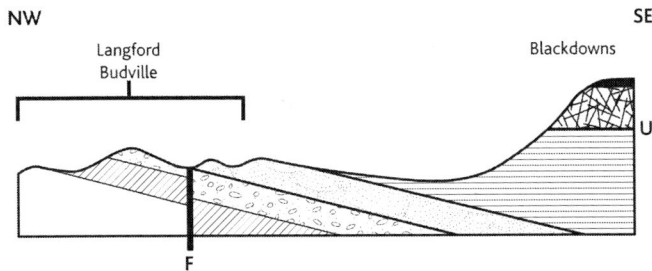

NW   SE

Langford   Blackdowns
Budville

Fig. 3 Schematic geological cross section (not to scale)
      F - Fault
      U - Unconformity

embedded in a calcareous matrix. The pebbles were extracted, crushed and mixed with the matrix before firing. The unwanted silica rich pebbles (mostly quartzite) were probably used as road stone. The nearest source for the well rounded limestone cobbles is the Mendip Hills, giving a clue perhaps to the size and power of some of the ephemeral Triassic rivers which deposited the beds.

Many of the spring-fed streams which drain from the parish eventually into the River Tone are in places quite deeply incised into small gorges. A study of the sediments exposed in these locations shows a chaotic jumble of pebbles, sand and clay with no discernable bedding. These deposits are the product of much more recent geomorphological activity, during the Pleistocene. Over the last 50,000 years Britain was subjected to the last glacial phase in a period of intense climatic cooling which ended around 10,000 years ago. Glaciers never reached Langford Budville but very low temperatures resulted in permafrost (permanently frozen subsoil) with a surface layer subject to intense freeze-thaw weathering and solifluction, where a saturated summer melt layer of sediment flowed downslope choking the river valleys. It is this material which is now being reworked by present day streams. Elsewhere solifluction material mantles the upper slopes, sometimes making it difficult to discern where the recent deposits end and the solid geology begins. This goes some way to explain why, in the Langford Budville area at least, the influence of geology on landscape is subtle, outcrops are few and the most productive way of studying the local geology is by observing the local architecture.

Appendix E

WEATHER PATTERNS

Climate data supplied by Simon Ratsey for some years weather correspondent for the *Wellington Weekly News*. He grew up near Spring Grove, starting his weather records there in 1960

Changes in Mean Annual Temperature in Britain: Bronze Age to Present

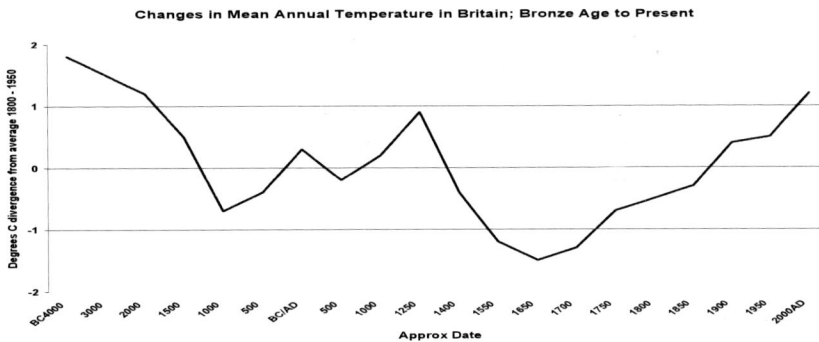

Changes in Mean Annual Temperature in Britain; Bronze Age to Present

(Please note that the time scale on the graph is not constant)

While the temperature variations may not look much, bear in mind that a mean annual temperature rise of 1°C is the equivalent to a move of two degrees of latitude nearer the Equator. In other words, like moving Taunton to the coast of Brittany.

Prehistoric Phase

Conditions in the distant past have been conjectured from "proxy" climate data, such as peat deposits, fossil pollen grains, buried soils and other archaeological finds. Figures are therefore approximate.

Britain and Western Europe enjoyed what has been termed the Climatic Optimum, roughly between 5000 – 2000BC. It was the warmest period since before the last glaciation. Neolithic and, later, Bronze Age settlements flourished on upland areas such as Exmoor and Dartmoor. Summer temperatures were probably more than 2°C warmer than today, and there was less rainfall.

Conditions deteriorated after about 2000BC, with temperatures lower and rainfall higher than average by about 1000BC. Upland areas were abandoned and peat bogs expanded, both on Exmoor and the Somerset Levels. Things were at their worst about the start of the Iron Age (500BC). Valley bottoms were badly drained and heavily wooded, so settlement was mostly on low hills. There was then a slight amelioration, which continued during the period of Roman occupation.

Early Historical Phase

While "proxy" climate data continue to be used, from Roman times onward there were increasing amounts of documentary evidence allowing climate at a particular time to be estimated. Literate people, especially priests, kept useful diaries from as early as the 14th century.

A deterioration in Britain's climate coincided almost precisely with the end of the period of Roman occupation, conditions being nearly as cool and wet in the Early Anglo-Saxon period as at the start of the Iron Age. Low lying, poorly drained areas were avoided, the preferred settlement sites being on gentle slopes with sandy soil, where it was possible to farm. Many of the villages in the Vale of Taunton Deane trace their origins to this time.

Temperatures generally rose in the Late Anglo-Saxon period, and for a couple of hundred years after the Norman Conquest. By the end of the 13th century, summers were drier and winters milder than at any time since the Late Neolithic period. The growing of cereals took place at altitudes not even achieved in World War II, and productive vineyards existed as far north as Cambridgeshire. It was a period of rural prosperity and population growth.

A rapid deterioration set in during the early 1300s, causing widespread famine before the Black Death arrived to further decimate the population later in the century. This heralded the onset of the "Little Ice Age", conditions becoming progressively cooler and wetter from the Tudor period onwards, and lasting until the end of the 17th century. The winter of 1683-84, recalled in R.D.Blackmore's *Lorna Doone* was the most severe on record.

Recent Historical Phase

From about 1700 we have instrumental records of rainfall and temperature that allow direct comparisons to be made, as well as many documentary sources of information such as the famous diaries of Gilbert White of Selborne.

Our climate warmed erratically through the 18th century, with a marked improvement in the mid 1700s, though the winter of 1740 was memorably severe. A series of major volcanic eruptions around the world were the probable cause of spells with cooler conditions, as dust in the upper atmosphere reduced solar radiation. There were some very cool, wet summers in the late 18th and early 19th centuries. 1816 became known as "The Year without a Summer", following the previous year's eruption of Mt. Tambora in the Philippines.

It was a difficult time for farming communities, and the combination of rural hunger and the growing demand for labour in the new coal-based industrial centres led to a decline in many villages across the country. (This trend would not be reversed until the latter part of the 20th century, when personal mobility allowed people to live in rural areas while working in a town or city.)

From the middle of the 19th century, we have seen the most significant rise in average temperatures since the early Mediæval period. This may be attributable in part to the increased levels of carbon dioxide in the earth's atmosphere, linked to the growing rate of burning of fossil fuels since the start of the Industrial Revolution. Average temperatures in Britain at the start of the 21st century are believed to be higher than at any time since the prehistoric Climatic Optimum.

Climatic Phases in England since 1880

1880 – 1949: First signs of warming

In the 1880s, March was generally the last month of winter, and most Aprils were colder than a typical March today. Summers were often cool and sometimes very damp, with only the occasional very hot, dry spell.

The 1890s saw a marked warming-up, but this was followed by a relapse in the first decade of the 20th century. Between 1900–1909 there were 6 very cold Februarys, the coldest May of the century (1903) and the equal coldest June (1909). There was only one really warm summer month in the last four years of the decade.

From 1910–1929 the warming process resumed, if erratically. The summer of 1911 was remarkably long and hot, while in 1912 from July onwards the weather was dire, following a major volcanic eruption in Alaska. Winters were generally fairly benign, apart from the long and bitter one of 1916–17. The summer of 1921 was hot and dry, with widespread water shortages, while those of 1924 and 1927 were exceptionally wet.

The 1930s were blessed with a series of fine summers, (1933–35), and the wettest July of the century (1936). Winters were rarely memorable, with few extremely low temperatures, although February 1933 saw widespread very heavy snowfall.

The 1940s saw some severe winters (notably the first three wartime winters, and that of 1947). Nevertheless, warm springs, some hot summers and fine autumns made it the warmest decade on record at the time.

1950 – 1979: A mid-century relapse

This period was probably the toughest for farmers since before World War I. The warming trend of the first half of the century came to an abrupt end.

Nearly every other winter was colder than normal, and there were 8 Februarys in the 'severe' category, notably that of 1956. Significant snowfall in January and February became the norm, although the winter of 1962-63 was a true record-breaker for duration of snow cover and low temperatures. There were other heavy snowfalls in this region during the 1960s and 1970s, the blizzard of February 1978 being the most noteworthy.

This period included some exceptionally wet spells, and historic floods (such as the Lynmouth flood of August 1952). The summers of 1954 and 1956 were cool and wet, and rated the worst in the 20th century. That of 1959, fine and dry from May to the end of September, was a remarkable exception to the rule, as the 1960s and early 1970s continued to be notably lacking in summer weather.

1960 included the wettest autumn on record, with the flooding of the River Tone preventing access to Wellington from the north. There were exceptional July rainstorms in 1968 and 1969, while June 1971 was notably cool and wet, only to be exceeded in that respect by June 1972. The harvest in 1974 was severely disrupted by continuous dull, damp weather.

In contrast, 1975 had the hottest summer since 1947, to be surpassed by 1976. Unprecedented heat in June scarcely diminished through July and August, crops shrivelled and Clatworthy Reservoir was two-thirds empty. Then almost a year's worth of rain fell in the next six months. What a time!

1980 onwards: Warming trend resumes

As a decade, the 1980s showed a slight cooling, thanks to some winters that compared with those of the 1950s, notably 1981/82, 1985, 1986 and 1987. Some scientists continued to speak of the 'global cooling' that had been a theme in the 1970s, with the summers of 1985, 1986 and 1988 being dismal.

In fact, overall, summers in the '80s were warmer than they had been since the 1940s, with some extremes of heat. July 1983 was at the time the warmest calendar month on record. The summers of 1982, 1984 and 1989 also included notably hot spells.

The non-existent winter of 1988–89 signalled a marked change to warmer conditions, with the increased frequency of early springs in the following two decades unprecedented in UK records. In the 1990s the average temperature for the summer half-year (April – September) was more than 1°C higher than in the 1950s, and warmer still in the first decade of the 21st century.

Since 1990, new records have been set in England for the average temperature for all months save December, March and June. Winter snows became a rarity. Long-term observations of nature suggested that spring was arriving earlier and autumn later.

This phase included extremes of rainfall and drought, with new monthly rainfall records for January, April, June, July and November. 1998–2002 was our wettest-ever 5 year spell, while 2003 was exceptionally dry. 2010 was also dry, with severe cold to start and end the year, to be followed by astonishing heat waves early and late in 2011, the warmest year on record in our region and also one of the driest.

Appendix F

CHANGING FACES – a history project in the making

Changing Faces – Langford Budville History Project was launched on 1st December 2009 at an informal meeting in The Function Room of the Martlet Inn when interested people initially gathered to share old photographs and memorabilia.

Aims of the project:
- *To collate memories and memorabilia/photographs of times gone by.*
- *To reflect on the history of the rural village of Langford Budville by researching and acknowledging the life and work of previous generations of inhabitants.*
- *To form an archive of material for future generations.*
- *To produce some form of non-profit making publication highlighting the important aspects of the 'changing faces' of the village.*

In the ensuing months requests were made in the Parish magazine for further information and soon an archive began to form. This enabled an exhibition to be mounted at the Village Fete in July 2010 and an opportunity to raise money to go towards the publication of a book.

On 30th November a second meeting was held in the Martlet to give people time to peruse the photographs assembled to date and help identify faces and locations.

The Village Fete in July 2011 was once again a vehicle for a display of material, this time enhanced by an excellent exhibition, mounted by Glyn Jones, of artefacts/tools used by his grandfather and father as wheelwrights, carpenters and undertakers.

On the 4th February 2012 a final gathering took place at The Martlet as a decision had been made to try and publish the book to commemorate Queen Elizabeth II Diamond Jubilee. This was therefore the last chance for people to see all the material that had been amassed before the process of compiling the actual book began. A record number of people came and more money was raised through a bring-and-buy sale and raffle to offset the expense of printing the book. A list of names of people who would be interested in buying a copy of the book when it was printed was added to. This helped inform the decision of how many books to print.

On all these above occasions it was heartening to also welcome people who didn't currently live in the village but who had spent part of their childhood here and who had travelled from Birmingham, Ilminster and Taunton to bring their findings and their memories – see photographs overleaf.

It is hoped that the book meets with most people's approval

The final history meeting in The Martlet, February 2012
Colleen Sanders, Christopher Fox, June Marshall, Alan Tucker, Valerie Pitman,
Glyn Jones, Roger Wotton – who spent their childhood in the village.

Robert and William Hayes – who spent many of their
school holidays in Langford Budville – 'down on the
farm'

Gerald Brewer – who has had a few
'tales' to tell about his life in Langford
Budville

Aerial photograph taken by the RAF on 11th July 1946, courtesy of English Heritage.

Wiveliscombe

Milverton

Chipley

Langford
Heathfield

Wellington

Bere Farm

Runnington

INDEX

Place Names

Family Names